What do you need?

A short quiz?
A take-home assignment?
Perhaps a challenging exercise for those certain students?
Then check out the Backpack CD!

Identify muscles

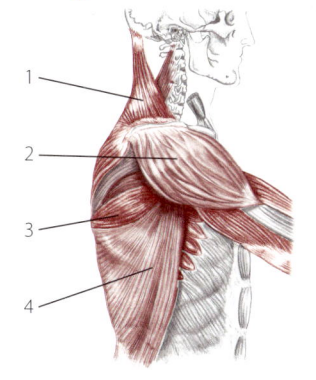

1
2
3
4

Word Finds

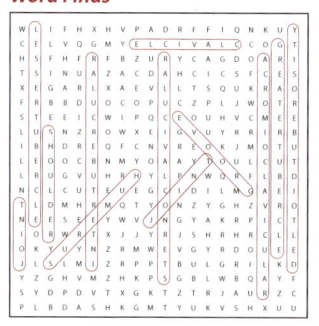

Muscles and Movements

Action

1) _____

Synergists

2) _____

3) _____

Antagonist

4) _____

Shorten or Lengthen?

1) Passive abduction of the scapula would _____ the middle fibers of the trapezius.

2) Passive elevation of the scapula would _____ the trapezius' upper fibers.

3) Passive rotation of the head to the left would _____ the left trapezius' upper fibers.

Matching
Match the origin and insertion to the correct muscle.

Origins
1) Lateral 1/3 of clavicle, acromion and spine of the scapula
2) Lateral side of inferior angle and lower 1/2 of lateral border

Insertions
3) Crest of the lesser tubercle of the humerus
4) Deltoid tuberosity

Muscle	O	I
Teres Major	___	___
Deltoid	___	___

Books of Discovery brings healthcare providers around the world the very best in palpatory and anatomical information. We are committed to providing quality educational products for students, instructors and practitioners.

Over the past ten years I have often remarked that our products offer more than "how to find muscles, bones and more." Our books, study aids and flashcards help a practitioner locate structures so they can apply their skills accurately.

It will always make us feel proud knowing that a mother in Portland, Maine or an athlete in Sarasota, Florida or even a bricklayer in Liverpool, England is receiving quality bodywork from a practitioner who has benefited from our products.

Andrew Biel

This **Instructor's Field Guide** is produced with vegetable-based ink and paper composed of 40% recycled stock and 10% post-consumer waste. Books of Discovery donates a portion of its profits to reforestation projects. Please visit www.yourtruenature.com for more information.

Trail Guide to the Body
How to locate the muscles, bones and more

Instructor's Field Guide

First Edition

Andrew Biel, LMP
Licensed Massage Practitioner

Contributors
Shelly Loewen
Lisa Nelson

Illustrations by Robin Dorn, LMP
Licensed Massage Practitioner

First Edition

THIS PRODUCT IS NOT FOR RESALE

Copyright © 2005 text, illustrations by Books of Discovery. All rights reserved. No part of this book may be reproduced in any form, or by any electronic, mechanical or other means, without prior permission in writing from the publisher.

Published by Books of Discovery
2539 Spruce St., Boulder, CO 80302 USA
www.booksofdiscovery.com
info@booksofdiscovery.com
800.775.9227

Associate Editor
Joan E. Ryan, LMT, MD

Printed in Canada by Printcrafters, Winnipeg

Library of Congress Cataloging-in-Publication Data

Biel, Andrew R.
Trail Guide to the Body: Instructor's Field Guide
First Edition

ISBN: 0-9658534-7-0
Library of Congress Control Number: 2005902121

15 14 13 12 11 10 9 8 7 6 5 4

Disclaimer
The purpose of Books of Discovery's products is to provide information for hands-on therapists on the subject of palpatory anatomy. This book does not offer medical advice to the reader and is not intended as a replacement for appropriate health care and treatment. For such advice, readers should consult a licensed physician.

Table of Contents

Introduction — 6
- Foreword — 7
- Field Guide Resources — 8
- Learning Objectives — 12
- Tips & Reminders for Students — 14
- Tips & Reminders for Instructors — 16
- Learning & Teaching Activities — 18

Shoulder & Arm — 24
- Topography — 25
- Skin & Fascia — 25
- Bones — 25
- Bony Landmark Trails — 26-27
- Muscles — 28-41
- Other Structures — 42

Forearm & Hand — 44
- Topography — 45
- Skin & Fascia — 45
- Bones — 45
- Bony Landmark Trails — 46-47
- Muscles — 48-61
- Other Structures — 62

Spine & Thorax — 64
- Topography — 65
- Skin & Fascia — 65
- Bones — 65
- Bony Landmark Trails — 66-67
- Muscles — 68-80
- Other Structures — 81

Head, Neck & Face — 82
- Topography — 83
- Skin & Fascia — 83
- Bones — 83
- Bony Landmark Trails — 84
- Muscles — 85-94
- Other Structures — 95

Pelvis & Thigh — 96
- Topography — 97
- Skin & Fascia — 97
- Bones — 97
- Bony Landmark Trails — 98-99
- Muscles — 100-112
- Other Structures — 113

Leg & Foot — 114
- Topography — 115
- Skin & Fascia — 115
- Bones — 115
- Bony Landmark Trails — 116-117
- Muscles — 118-129
- Other Structures — 130

Synergists List — 132
Glossary of Terms — 138
Pronunciation and Etymology — 142

1 Introduction to Field Guide

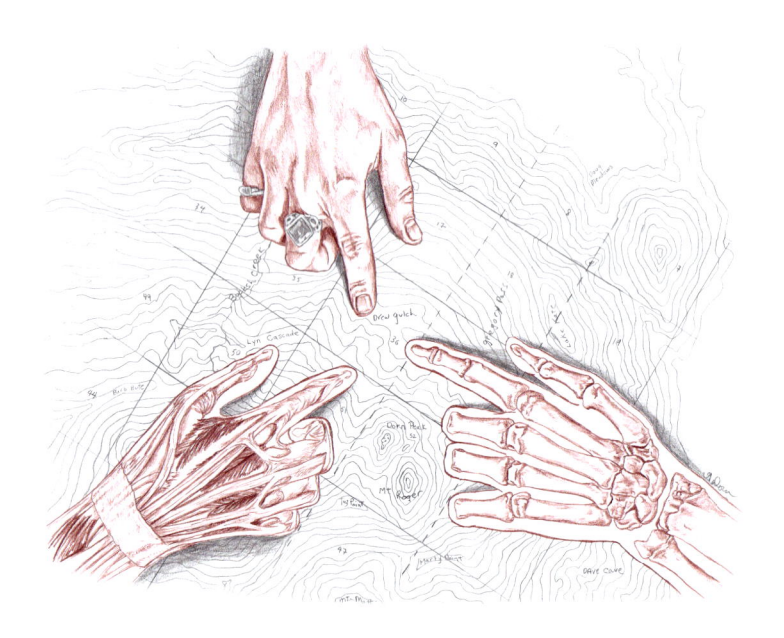

Foreword	7
Field Guide Resources	8
Learning Objectives	12
Tips and Reminders for Students	14
Tips and Reminders for Instructors	16
Learning & Teaching Activities	18

Foreword

Have you ever found yourself in the middle of a classroom lesson, staring at the students and wondering, "What do I do now?" You thought you were prepared, but then, at that awful moment, realized you weren't. Mary Poppins remarked, "Well begun, half done," and this tenet is certainly true of teaching.

Welcome to the *Instructor's Field Guide*. Whether you are a new instructor or an experienced teacher who has recently been introduced to *Trail Guide to the Body*, this guide will help you to prepare for leading students through palpatory anatomy lessons. With exercises, insights and lesson tips, the *Field Guide* lets you choose the tools that you will need to prepare for the teaching and learning adventures that lie ahead.

This *Field Guide* resource package (this book and the Backpack CD) allows you easy access to helpful, relevant material. It includes outlines, lesson plans, quiz questions, teaching hints, visual aids, assessment tools and much more. You can pick and choose from these tools based on your level of expertise, personal needs and preferences.

The ultimate goal of the *Instructor's Field Guide* resource package is to help you design and implement a solid lesson of palpatory anatomy, but not to tell you what to do or how to teach. The package contains a myriad of suggestions intended to help you capitalize on who *you* are, how *you* learn and how *you* teach. Just as a teacher supports her students, the *Instructor's Field Guide* will support you, the teacher.

Field Guide Resources

The *Instructor's Field Guide* is a multimedia package that includes this book, the Backpack CD and the Palpation DVD. Whether you are attracted to books or enjoy accessing computerized information, the following is an overview of what you can find in these unique teaching tools.

Instructor's Field Guide

Using the Book

This Introduction chapter contains general tips for teaching palpation, learning and teaching activities that can be incorporated into your lesson plans and an overview of assessment skills that can be used both in and outside of the classroom. The bulk of this book, however, offers material that corresponds with both the chapters and structures of *Trail Guide to the Body*.

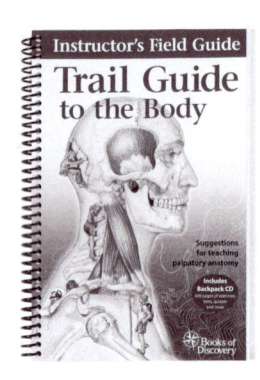

A) **Name of Structure**

B) **Mini Flashcards**
   Similar to *Trail Guide Flashcards*, these squares contain the **O**rigin, **I**nsertion, **A**ction and **N**erve innervation information for each muscle.

C) **Starter Questions**
   These basic questions are designed to help you either assess students' knowledge of the material scheduled for the day's lesson or introduce students to *Trail Guide* information that will be covered in that lesson.

D) **Activities of Daily Living (ADL)**
   This section contains a short list of daily activities that can be used to help students familiarize themselves with the movements that are made possible by each muscle. You may already have a list of your favorite ADLs or want to ask your students to create a list of their own.

E) **Two Cents**
   Although two cents doesn't buy much, we think these simple tips and reminders are worth their weight in gold. Hopefully they can help you avoid some of the not-so-obvious pitfalls that come with the territory when teaching palpatory anatomy.

F) **Tables**
   Corresponding reference page numbers to *Trail Guide*, the *Student Handbook*, the Backpack CD and the Palpation DVD can be found at the bottom of the page.

Brachioradialis

A
- Flex the elbow (humeroulnar joint)
- Assist in pronation and supination of the forearm when these movements are resisted

O Lateral supracondylar ridge of humerus

I Styloid process of radius

N Radial

Starter Questions
- How many muscles supinate the forearm and what are they? *(Three: biceps brachii, supinator and brachioradialis)*
- This muscle serves as a dividing line between which two muscle groups? *(flexors and extensors of the wrist and hand)*
- Which joint(s) does this muscle cross? *(humeroulnar/humeroradial - the elbow, but not the radiocarpal - the wrist)*

ADL
- Turning a door handle or screwdriver
- Combing your hair
- Bringing a beer stein up to one's mouth

Two Cents
- This is often a fun muscle for students to explore - highly visible and palpable.
- Acknowledge for students that the distal half of the belly is far less distinguishable than the bulkier, proximal portion.
- Consider starting students at the radial tuberosity and sliding proximally to feel the flat tendon enlarge into the belly.

TGB, 3rd p. 141	Backpack Forearm & Hand	Handbook p. 69-70	DVD Forearm & Hand

Introduction 9

⛰ Field Guide Backpack CD

Every hiker needs a good backpack, even if only to carry the basic essentials like food, water and the occasional tube of sunscreen. The Backpack CD is designed in a similar fashion and contains some of the basic essentials for teaching with *Trail Guide to the Body*.

Most importantly, it contains the **Backpack Test and Quiz Bank**. With more than 400 illustrated question pages and 800 multiple-choice questions, this collection contains a variety of tools that can be offered to students as in-class assessments, homework assignments or general content evaluations.

Just insert the Backpack CD into your computer's CD drive and the Backpack's Main Menu window will appear on the screen. This window will display the major sections of the Test and Quiz Bank:

- Introduction/Navigating the Body
- Shoulder & Arm
- Forearm & Hand
- Spine & Thorax
- Head, Neck & Face
- Pelvis & Thigh
- Leg & Foot

Some of the question types include:

- diagrams for students to label
- matching origins with insertions
- shortened and lengthened muscle questions
- crossword puzzles
- word find puzzles
- palpation fill-in questions
- multiple-choice questions

The Backpack CD contains additional teaching information, including two generic lesson plans, 10 in-class learning activities and a resource list.

♠ DVD - 54 Essential Muscles

Trail Guide to the Body DVD: Palpation Guide to 54 Essential Muscles, is a resource for both students and instructors. The video closely parallels the presentation of muscles (and related structures) in *Trail Guide*. Clint Chandler, American Massage Therapy Association Teacher of the Year, leads the learner in specific palpation techniques to locate, identify and palpate fifty-four muscles on a variety of models.

The DVD can assist students in pre-viewing muscles before class and in reviewing to prepare for practice and testing. For an instructor, the DVD will be valuable for reviewing palpatory techniques prior to a class, preparing a teacher-in-training or as a refresher for long-forgotten material.

The menu format allows the viewer to quickly navigate to the muscle that he or she would like to see demonstrated. It also allows the viewer to "freeze" the action at any point without a loss of image quality or watch the action in "slow motion."

In keeping with the spirit of *Trail Guide*, the video is both fun and loaded with accurate anatomical information. This DVD will allow your students to "hit the ground running" and allow you more time for effective one-on-one tableside teaching, guidance and encouragement.

Learning Objectives

Whether you are teaching musculoskeletal anatomy (mostly origins, insertions and actions), more complex movement or kinesiology courses, you might find it helpful to refer to the student learning objectives listed below. They can assist you to map out a lesson plan or set guidelines for assessing your students' knowledge and skills.

Learning Objectives for Musculoskeletal Anatomy may include:

For each bone or bony landmark, students will be able to:
- Name and locate the bone on a diagram, skeleton and classmate
- Name and locate the specific bony landmark on a diagram, skeleton and classmate
- Palpate each of the bones and specific landmarks on a variety of classmates

For each muscle, students will be able to:
- Name and locate the muscle on a diagram, skeleton and classmate
- Describe the location of the muscle in relationship to other muscles
- Name and locate the origin and insertion of each muscle on a diagram, skeleton and classmate
- Superficially outline the shape and fiber direction of each muscle
- Palpate the length of each muscle (from origin to insertion) on a variety of classmates
- Clearly distinguish the muscle from its surrounding structures on a variety of classmates
- Demonstrate the actions of the muscle

For each additional structure, students will be able to:
- Name and locate the structure on a diagram, skeleton and classmate
- Describe the relationship of the structure to the bones, bony landmarks and/or muscles

Additional Learning Objectives for Movement Courses (Kinesiology) may include:

For each muscle, students will be able to:
- Name and locate the muscle's synergists
- Name and locate the muscle's antagonists
- Identify Activities of Daily Living (ADL) that involve the muscle
- Demonstrate a passive position of this muscle in a shortened and lengthened state
- Demonstrate an appropriate isometric resistive (resisted contraction) for the muscle
- Demonstrate an appropriate stretch for the muscle
- Demonstrate an appropriate reciprocal inhibition for the muscle
- Identify the impact on posture this muscle would have if it were chronically shortened
- Identify the impact on posture this muscle would have if it were chronically lengthened

> *Trail Guide to the Body* is 422 pages of dense information. Sitting down with your colleagues and identifying what material from the book is vital to your program and what will not be addressed is a good way to prepare for the courses.

Tips & Reminders for Students

Just as a golf instructor might recommend a particular club, stance or swing, you have the opportunity to offer students a few tips and reminders as they develop their palpation skills. These simple, seemingly obvious cues can turn a potentially frustrating situation (such as not being able to locate a specific structure) into an inspirational moment that motivates students to keep practicing.

Breathe
Stress happens - especially during learning experiences. Breathing supports relaxation and, besides keeping us alive, makes it possible for us to learn.

Be Receptive
Palpation is more than just locating a structure. It is about exploring its placement, shape, texture and the relationship it has with surrounding structures. Try closing your eyes. Now allow your hands and fingers to experience the contours, temperature and structures of your partner's body. This can bring new discoveries to your awareness while allowing your hands to "see."

Soft and Sensitive
Reaching different structures - at various levels of palpation - is not accomplished through pressure but rather through intention. To gain depth, try placing one of your hands on top of the other, using the top hand to create pressure and stability while the bottom hand stays soft and sensitive to the tissues below. A slow and soft hand can help you move deeper into the tissue and reach structures more easily.

Just Because You Were Born With A Trapezius…
…doesn't mean that you will be able to locate it on yourself or on another person's body the first time you try. Be patient and keep trying. You might even find that making a wrong turn or getting lost will actually help you find what you are looking for.

Sculpting, Rolling and Strumming
Making full hand contact and sculpting (accessing all sides and edges of a muscle or bone) can help you define its shape and its relationship with surrounding structures. Rolling your fingers or thumb *across* rather than *along* the surface of a bone can help outline a structure's shape. When ascertaining the direction of a muscle's fibers or its tensile state, try strumming the muscle.

Reading Aloud
Just like learning a new language, hearing the words from *Trail Guide* as you read out loud increases your learning and retention.

Consult With Your Student Partners
Your fellow classmates are guinea pigs who are happy to share. Inquire about your pressure, depth and your palpation skills in general.

Sensitive Areas
Although it may go without saying, regions such as the groin and axilla require a slow, deliberate touch.

Changing Position
Your "supine" partner can turn over or lay on his side; different positions allow for better access to palpate certain structures.

Self-Palpation
Palpating yourself can make it easier to locate structures on others. Besides, your body is the one cheat sheet you can bring along during tests and quizzes.

Tips & Reminders for Instructors

Unlike subjects that lend themselves to more of a lecture presentation, palpatory anatomy is best facilitated by teachers-turned-tour-guides. As a teacher, you have the opportunity to lead students on a journey. You can direct students' efforts and watch for those who lag behind. You can also initiate teamwork among students and help the class travel as a strong, cohesive group. Whether helping students who lack energy or simply need assurance that they are on the "right" path, you have much to consider and do while guiding students to their final destination.

Words of encouragement and respect from a teacher can promote the perfect climate for students to study, learn and grow. Like students, teachers can also benefit from a little guidance when they enter the classroom. Whether these tips are new to you or reflect your expertise, consider them food for thought as you facilitate your students' learning process.

Starting On The Right Foot
Most students approach their first class with a healthy mixture of excitement and anxiety. It is important to provide them with accurate information about who you are as a teacher and what will be expected of them as students. Consider designing your first session in a way that provides students with what they need to succeed both in and outside of the classroom.

A Quiet Example
Since palpation is a kinesthetic experience, you might consider spending a few minutes before class (while students are filtering into the room) gently stretching your body. Musing informally about your last class or posing warm-up questions while reaching for the ceiling or stretching your low back invites students to join in as they choose. Your example will speak volumes - demonstrating to students one way that they can take care of their bodies and warm up their brains at the same time.

Give Them What Their Hands Need
Providing your students with time to review earlier information will deepen their initial encounters and build their confidence for later experiences. Be sure to provide your students with opportunities to repeat and review palpatory experiences.

Faking It
Some palpation exercises can be nebulous and discouraging. Not wanting to look incompetent or slow the class down, students will fake it, "Oh, yeah. I feel it…sure." This is understandable, but not acceptable or useful. Students need to know from you that it is safe for them to admit what they do not know. Create an encouraging environment where students can share their learning, their confusion and ask "dumb" questions.

The Panic-Poke Response
Students with limited palpatory experience may have difficulty locating certain landmarks or structures. In their frantic attempt to locate something - anything - they begin to squeeze, rub or poke their partner's body tissue. Students often jab and mash their partners unmercifully until they locate something that resembles the intended structure. When this occurs, ask the student to step away from the table, take a few deep breaths and return to the palpatory exercise.

Challenge
Giving students a chance to try something new helps them expand their horizons, build their confidence and remind them that there is more than one way to palpate a structure. Challenging students to try less popular techniques - fingers instead of thumbs or supine instead of prone - adds depth to their understanding and skill.

Patience
It is easy for practitioners and teachers to forget what it was like to be a novice. Pushing students to learn too much information too quickly or in a way that satisfies your classroom agenda can hinder successful learning. Teachers who can demonstrate patience and compassion during the learning process not only create a safe and supportive learning environment, but model qualities that will be emulated by their students in the classroom and beyond.

A Good Start and a Strong Finish
Students tend to remember the first and the last moments in class. That said, consider beginning class by introducing the topic of the day followed by outlining the activities that will help students learn and execute that plan. At the end of class, include 5-10 minutes for student questions, and use those inquiries to review the information covered throughout the session. Ending class in this way will place an exclamation mark where a question mark or period otherwise might have been.

Sticky Tissue
Dense, adhered tissue can challenge the palpatory skills of even the most experienced practitioner. If this occurs in class, shift the palpating student to another partner where he can continue to practice the exercise. Then bring him back to his original partner to apply his new skills. This way he can gain insight into the differences of tissues while developing confidence as a practitioner.

Frustration and Learning
Fear, doubt and feelings of frustration are all part of the learning process. Although frustration does not prevent learning, it does intensify the experience and sometimes camouflages other feelings below the surface. Meeting with a student who appears overwhelmed or confused gives you a chance to engage with him about his progress and provides you with insight into what's really going on. This makes it possible for you to offer him guidance or refer him to tutoring programs or other out-of-class resources that can help him achieve success.

Learning & Teaching Activities

It's been said that we teach the way that we learn. This implies that we bring ourselves into the classroom, flavoring the lessons we create, the assessments we offer and the activities we choose. Regardless of your personal preferences, your task as a teacher is to develop learning tools that will help *all* of your students learn professional skills and grow as practitioners-in-training.

Keep in mind that your students' personal preferences and learning needs are as diverse as yours. Given the potential for such diversity, it's safe to say that a teacher could feel overwhelmed. If that is the case, begin reflecting on your own learning experience, and simply begin teaching from there. Once you get your bearings, you can tailor your approach to your students' learning needs one day at a time.

Traditional Learning Methods

There are a number of traditional learning methods that can be implemented both in and outside of the classroom. While some of these methods involve familiar tools like books, flashcards and overhead transparencies, the way you introduce or utilize them can make the difference between inspiring students to learn and an activity that was doomed to fail from the start.

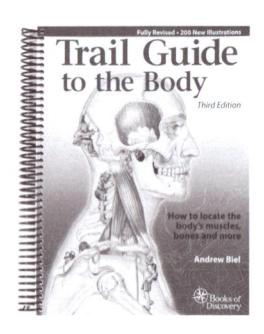

Reading Assignments

You prepare for class, so try using reading assignments as preparatory work for your students. To help them get the most out of *Trail Guide to the Body*, encourage students to read the opening paragraphs and familiarize themselves with new words and structures while checking side boxes for additional information. This way, even if they skim the text, they will be focusing on what's most important.

Also, tell your students *why* they should spend time reading the material. Remind them that familiarizing themselves with the words and techniques articulated in print will prime them for a smooth and successful learning experience.

Trail Guide to the Body Flashcards

While this tool is designed to help students learn anatomy in a fun and easy way, *Trail Guide Flashcards* can help you facilitate a lesson on the same material. At the risk of sounding like a 30-second infomercial, these flashcards contain the **A**, **O**, **I** and **N** information of each muscle and page references that direct students to more information in *Trail Guide*. Frankly, the more often your students see you use the flashcards in the classroom, the more they will use them on their own.

18 Instructor's Field Guide

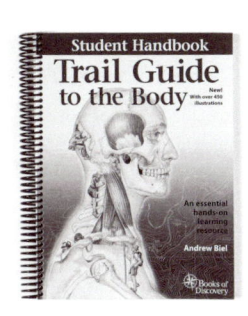

Student Handbook
This interactive workbook is designed to provide students with numerous ways to test their knowledge from *Trail Guide*. It contains various question types including fill-in-the-blank, illustrations to color, matching origins and insertions, muscle movements and palpatory journal exercises. Students might find it helpful if you assign pages from the workbook for an upcoming class or an exam review.

Visual Aids
Since palpation is a kinesthetic activity, it is important to find a balance between lecture and hands-on practice. Consider having students pair up and palpate while you display *Trail Guide* overhead transparencies or PowerPoint slides while you speak to the class. This allows students to simultaneously practice palpation while connecting to visual and verbal information of the same structures.

Skeletons
When presented alone, bony landmarks appear to have no purpose, thus making it impossible for students to recognize their value and importance. In contrast, bones and bony landmarks are best understood when the muscles that attach to them are presented in conjunction with each landmark. Why not invite students to locate and palpate landmarks on the skeleton? Using ropes, fabric or rubber bands as muscles and attaching them to the muscle's **O** and **I** landmarks can help students make connections between landmarks and muscle attachments.

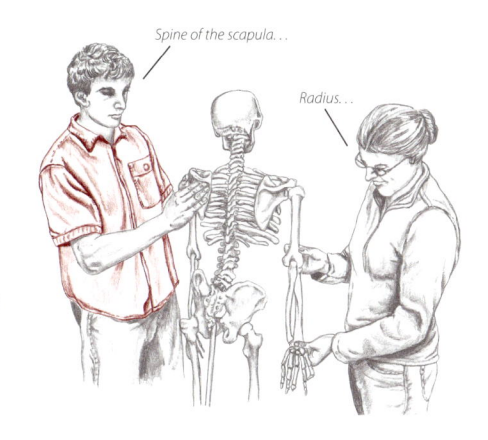

Introduction 19

⚕ Out-of-the-Box Activities

If your students' learning needs are outside your comfort or creative zone, take heart; there are a myriad of things you can do to support student success. The exercises, teaching/learning ideas and specific questions both in the *Field Guide* and Backpack CD can help you prepare for teaching palpatory anatomy without feeling stretched beyond your limits. Consider creating your own plan, starting with the tools and exercises that work best for you.

Coloring

Coloring is not just for kids. It is a helpful kinesthetic exercise with a big visual pay-off. Working alone or in groups, students can color diagrams or each other's bodies. With a minimum of supplies, you can facilitate a creative and powerful learning experience in the classroom that students can repeat during their own study time. Here are some variations:

Illustrations
Provide illustrations of muscle groups and allow students to color each muscle of the group with a different colored pen or pencil.

Skeletal Diagrams
Option #1: Provide a skeletal drawing and ask students to shade the areas of each muscle's **O**rigin and **I**nsertion. (Ask the students to make the origins one color and the insertions another.)

Option #2: Provide a skeletal drawing (full or partial skeleton) and instruct students to draw the muscles in the correct locations.

Body Coloring
Provide washable markers or paints and ask students to draw muscles or landmarks on their partners. A word to the wise: When planning an exercise that includes drawing muscles, landmarks or other structures on students' arms or legs, make sure that those markers are water-based and come off with a warm, soapy rinse. Trust me, you don't want your students leaving the classroom looking like a walking Picasso.

Color-on-Transparencies
Display skeletal transparencies or slides onto a whiteboard and have students color the muscles on the board one by one. Display the overheads from deeper to more superficial muscles, and place them in such a way that the muscles can be colored and overlapped to demonstrate the relationship of muscles in a group.

Life-Size Drawings
Provide a group of students with a large piece of butcher paper, and have them create life-size drawings of bones and muscles.

Choral Palpation
The study of palpation involves the foreign languages of anatomical terminology. For some students it is the *language* that makes the task of learning even origins and insertions seem impossible. That said, instead of asking students to memorize a heap of anatomical facts, engage their voices and hands to work together and create a multisensory experience.

This is a simple exercise that offers students a chance to practice vocalizing the terminology as they palpate a structure. This activity allows them to connect the names of each structure to their tactile location while developing teamwork with those in their small group.

Directions:
1. Divide the class into pairs or triads. One student will be on the table while the other student(s) will be palpating throughout the exercise.
2. Remind students that they will be working at a pace that you set as the choral director and that they will be asked to repeat key terminology as a group (or choir) as you direct their palpation.
3. Review and read aloud the palpation instructions for a **bony landmark trail** (from *Trail Guide*) so that the students can hear the information.
4. When you come to the name of a structure, ask all the students (clients and practitioners alike) to repeat the name of the landmark in unison - just like a choir - and have the practitioners palpate that landmark at their individual tables.
5. Check to see that each practitioner has accurately located the landmark. Then ask the class to repeat the name of the structure again while their hand(s) are still in position.
6. Continue on the trail until completion, then have the students trade roles and repeat the exercise.

Once the students are certain of the bony landmarks, you can vary the exercise by palpating **muscle origins and insertions**. Steps 1-2 are the same as above; steps 3-8 are below:
3. Recite the name of a muscle and ask all the students to repeat that name aloud.
4. State the origin of that muscle, asking all the students to repeat it aloud as the practitioners palpate for the origin at their individual tables.

5. Check to see that each practitioner has accurately located the origin. Then ask the class to repeat the name of the origin again while their hand(s) are still in position.
6. Request that the practitioners keep one hand on the origin and then recite the name of the insertion. Ask all the students to repeat the term aloud as the practitioners explore for that insertion site.
7. Check to see that each practitioner has accurately located the insertion. Then ask the class to repeat the name of the insertion once again while the practitioners' hands are still in position.
8. At this point, each practitioner should have one hand on the muscle's origin and one hand on the insertion. You may want to recite each piece of information again and ask them to repeat it out loud in unison.

Round Robin

Practicing palpation on a variety of body types is imperative for the development of solid hands-on skills. The round robin exercise is an indispensable learning activity that gives students the chance to instantly feel the differences between bodies.

Directions:
1. Make sure that the massage tables are arranged in a way that allows practitioners to move easily from one table to the next.
2. Ask students to partner-up and find a table. One student will be on the table as the "client" while the other is the "practitioner."
3. Have the practitioners palpate a specific structure on their clients (e.g., the tibialis anterior). Encourage the practitioners to get a sense of the size, texture and tension of the muscle.
4. Request that the practitioners shift clockwise to the next table in a round robin fashion and explore the same structure on their new client. (Paper towels and antibacterial gel should be used between partners.) Ask the practitioners if they notice any differences between the two individuals they have palpated.
5. Finally, have the practitioners move once again and repeat step 3.

Dissection

Some students have difficulty identifying and sensing the palpatory differences between various types of tissue. They know the names - bone, muscle, tendon, ligament, etc., but their awareness doesn't go beyond that. If you don't have access to a human cadaver lab, consider visiting your friendly neighborhood butcher shop and acquiring a few choice tissue samples. With the help of some rubber gloves and a warning to those with squeamish tendencies, you can facilitate a great learning experience for your students.

Directions:
1. At the butcher shop: Ask the butcher for a few large pieces of carcass (parts that would typically be thrown away). After a few strange looks, he will most likely provide you with chunks from the appendage and joint of a pig or steer.
2. In the classroom: Lay down large sheets of butcher paper, split the class into groups of 3-5, provide rubber gloves to all students and then proceed to lead them through a mini-cadaver course. Using a small scalpel, students can pull the tissues apart to find muscle, tendon, ligament, fibrous membrane, fascia and vascular structures. This 30-minute exercise will transform a student's attitude, comprehension and visual understanding of the body's tissues.

Lecture and Palpate

Lectures introducing muscles can oftentimes become bogged down with anatomical jargon. Instead, consider leading students through your verbal lecture as they kinesthetically see and feel the muscles.

Directions:
1. Separate students into pairs and have them identify who will be the client and who will be the practitioner.
2. As you display overheads and lead the discussion, ask the practitioner to palpate and observe as the client performs an assigned activity that requires specific muscles to work (e.g., plantar flexing on one's toes).
3. While palpating the posterior leg, the practitioner should feel and see the gastrocnemius and soleus work as the client performs the same activity several times.
4. Ask the practitioners to describe their observations such as changes in shape, tone and definition of the muscle.
5. Have the partners change roles and repeat the exercise using the same or different movements.

2 Shoulder & Arm

Topography	25
Skin & Fascia	25
Bones	25
Bony Landmark Trails	26-27
Muscles	28-41
Other Structures	42

Topography

| TGB, 3rd p. 54 | Handbook p. 25 |

Skin & Fascia

| TGB, 3rd p. 55 |

Bones

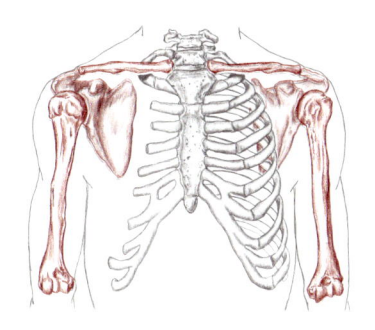

| TGB, 3rd p. 56-58 | Handbook p. 26-29 |

Starter Questions
- What three bones comprise the shoulder complex? *(scapula, humerus, clavicle)*
- Which joint is the single attachment site between the upper appendicular and axial skeletons? *(sternoclavicular joint)*
- By the way, how many people in class have broken their clavicle?

Two Cents
- The following list includes the bony landmarks and structures not introduced in *Trail Guide's* Shoulder & Arm chapter, but are mentioned in the origin and insertion information for some of the shoulder and arm muscles. It might be worthwhile to briefly introduce the names and locations of these structures beforehand.

    external occipital protuberance *(trapezius)*
    superior nuchal line *(trapezius)*
    ligamentum nuchae *(trapezius)*
    spinous processes of vertebrae *(trapezius and others)*
    thoracolumbar aponeurosis *(latissimus dorsi)*
    transverse processes of cervical vertebrae *(levator scapula)*
    tuberosity of radius *(biceps brachii)*
    olecranon process *(triceps brachii)*

Bony Landmark Trails

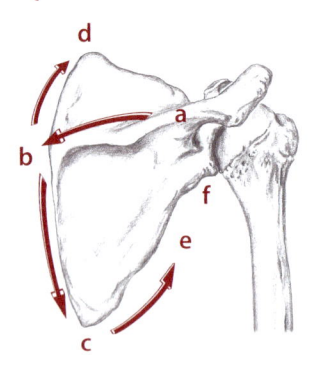

Trail 1 "Along the Edges" explores the sides and corners of the posterior scapula.

- **a** Spine of the scapula
- **b** Medial border
- **c** Inferior angle
- **d** Superior angle
- **e** Lateral border
- **f** Infraglenoid tubercle

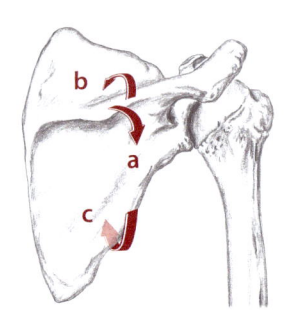

Trail 2 "In the Trenches" leaps off the spine of the scapula and sinks into the three basins of the scapula.

- **a** Infraspinous fossa
- **b** Supraspinous fossa
- **c** Subscapular fossa

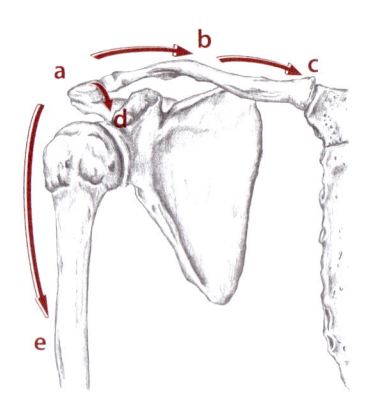

Trail 3 "Springboard Ledge" leads around to the anterior shoulder, using the scapula's acromion as a jumping-off point.

- **a** Acromion
- **b** Clavicle
- **c** Acromioclavicular and sternoclavicular joints
- **d** Coracoid process
- **e** Deltoid tuberosity

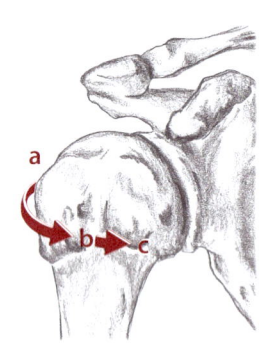

Trail 4 "Two Hills and a Valley" focuses on the three landmarks located along the anterior, proximal humerus.

- **a** Greater tubercle
- **b** Intertubercular groove
- **c** Lesser tubercle

26 Instructor's Field Guide

Bony Landmark Trails

Starter Questions
- As the spine of the scapula progresses laterally to the top of the shoulder it becomes which bony landmark? *(acromion)*
- The names of the three scapular fossaes give a big hint to what muscles lay in each of the basins. Can you name the muscles? *(supraspinatus, infraspinatus, subscapularis)*
- What three bony landmarks surround the infraspinous fossa? *(medial and lateral borders, spine of the scapula)*

Two Cents
- If you get lost while palpating, return to the spine of the scapula for a fresh start.
- Consider a pre-palpation demo before sending students off to explore their partners' subscapular fossae.

TGB, 3rd
p. 59-68

Muscles of the Shoulder & Arm

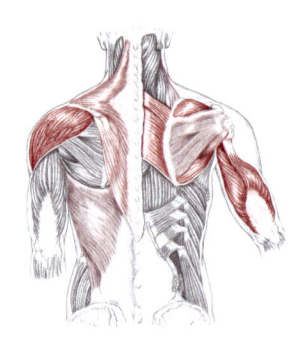

	Field Guide	TGB, 3rd ed.
Biceps Brachii	39	103
Coracobrachialis	41	107
Deltoid	29	75
Latissimus Dorsi	31	79
Levator Scapula	35	91
Pectoralis Major	37	97
Pectoralis Minor	38	100
Rotator Cuff Muscles	32	82
Rhomboid Major and Minor	34	90
Serratus Anterior	36	94
Teres Major	31	79
Trapezius	30	76
Triceps Brachii	40	105

Starter Questions

- Looking at the muscles of the shoulder and arm, can you identify an example of a convergent muscle? *(deltoid, trapezius, latissimus dorsi, pectoralis major, infraspinatus)*
- Which muscles appear to be virtually superficial? *(trapezius, deltoid, latissimus dorsi, pectoralis major)*
- Are there any tricks you can think of to remember the name of a muscle?

TGB, 3rd p. 69-74	Backpack Shoulder & Arm	Handbook p. 30-38	DVD Shoulder & Arm

Deltoid

A *All fibers:*
- Abduct the shoulder (g/h joint)

Anterior fibers:
- Flex the shoulder
- Medially rotate the shoulder
- Horizontally adduct the shoulder

Posterior fibers:
- Extend the shoulder
- Laterally rotate the shoulder
- Horizontally abduct the shoulder

O Lateral one-third of clavicle, acromion and spine of scapula

I Deltoid tuberosity

N Axillary from brachial plexus

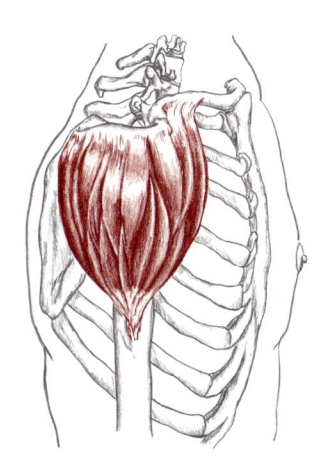

Starter Questions
- (While using overhead of deltoid): What information about the deltoid can you gather from looking at this overhead? *(convergent, attaches all three bones of shoulder together, has a wide variety of movement, superficial)*
- What bony landmarks could help you to isolate the deltoid? *(shaft of clavicle, acromion, spine of scapula, deltoid tuberosity)*

ADL
- Virtually all movements that involve the glenohumeral joint
- Raising a hand to ask a question
- Installing an overhead lightbulb

Two Cents
- Anyone can get their hands on the deltoid. That's easy. However, isolating its sides and tendinous ends can be challenging. Encourage students to "map out" the entire muscle with their fingers.
- Chances are that students will be new to the concept of synergists and antagonists, and compounding this is the fact that the deltoid is an antagonist to itself. Before you explain it to students, consider asking them how the deltoid could possibly move the shoulder in so many different directions. If they're still not getting it, use the skeleton: "Imagine there's a little guy standing here on the clavicle. He throws a rope down and hooks it on to the deltoid tuberosity. As he starts pulling . . ."

TGB, 3rd p. 75-76	Backpack Shoulder & Arm	Handbook p. 39-40	DVD Shoulder & Arm

Trapezius

A *Upper Fibers:*
  Bilaterally
    Extend the head and neck

  Unilaterally
    Laterally flex the head and neck to the same side
    Rotate the head and neck to the opposite side
    Elevate the scapula (scapulothoracic joint)
    Upwardly rotate the scapula (s/t joint)

  Middle Fibers:
    Adduct the scapula (s/t joint)
    Stabilize the scapula (s/t joint)

  Lower Fibers:
    Depress the scapula (s/t joint)
    Upwardly rotate the scapula (s/t joint)

O External occipital protuberance, medial portion of superior nuchal line of occiput, ligamentum nuchae and spinous processes of C-7 through T-12

I Lateral one-third of clavicle, acromion and spine of the scapula

N Spinal accessory and cervical plexus

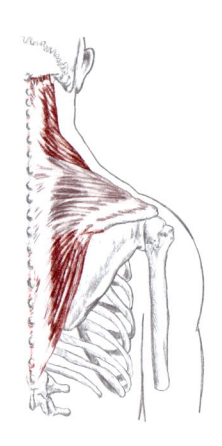

Starter Questions
- What do the trapezius and deltoid have in common regarding their attachments on the scapula? *(the trap's insertion is the same as the deltoid's origin)*
- Can you name another muscle that also adducts and elevates the scapula? *(rhomboids)*

ADL
- When Lance Armstrong extends his neck to see over the handlebars of his bike
- Holding a phone to your ear
- Carrying articles strapped across the shoulder (luggage, backpack, purse)

Two Cents
- Like the deltoid, the trapezius comes quickly into the hands. But that's only the upper/middle fibers that span the top of the neck. Students become less confident with the upper and lower portions. Reassure them that this muscle is 100% superficial and literally right below their fingers.

TGB, 3rd p. 76-78	Backpack Shoulder & Arm	Handbook p. 39-40	DVD Shoulder & Arm

Instructor's Field Guide

Latissimus Dorsi and Teres Major

Latissimus Dorsi

A
- Extend the shoulder (glenohumeral joint)
- Adduct the shoulder (g/h joint)
- Medially rotate the shoulder (g/h joint)

O Spinous processes of last six thoracic vertebrae, last three or four ribs, thoracolumbar aponeurosis and posterior iliac crest

I Crest of the lesser tubercle of the humerus

N Thoracodorsal

Teres Major

A
- Extend the shoulder (glenohumeral joint)
- Adduct the shoulder (g/h joint)
- Medially rotate the shoulder (g/h joint)

O Lateral side of inferior angle and lower half of lateral border of scapula

I Crest of the lesser tubercle of the humerus

N Lower subscapular

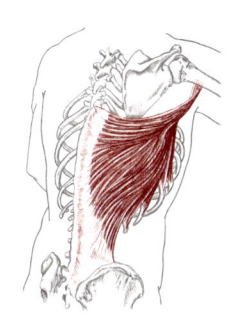

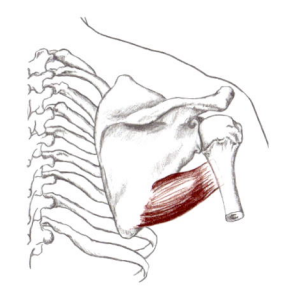

Starter Questions
- Can you name some athletes who have highly developed lats? *(rowers; swimmers - breast stroke; gymnasts - iron cross, parallel and high bar moves)*
- What is the teres major's nickname? *(lat's little helper)*

ADL
- Rowing with an oar
- Climbing up a rope
- Walking with crutches (hopefully not a daily activity)
- Unzipping the zipper down the back of your dress

Two Cents
- Consider reminding students that the portion of the latissimus that is easily accessible in the axillary region is only a small portion of the muscle. There's much more to be found.

TGB, 3rd p. 79-81	Backpack Shoulder & Arm	Handbook p. 39-40	DVD Shoulder & Arm

Shoulder & Arm

Rotator Cuff Muscles

Supraspinatus

A
- Abduct the shoulder (glenohumeral joint)
- Stabilize head of humerus in glenoid cavity

O Supraspinous fossa of scapula

I Greater tubercle of humerus

N Suprascapular

Supraspinatus

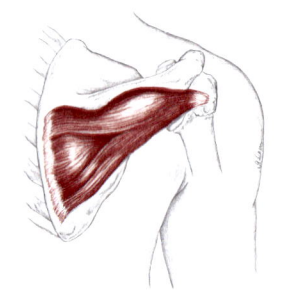

Infraspinatus

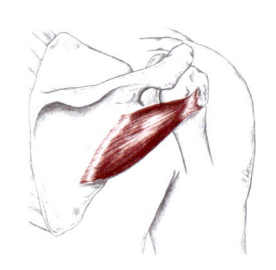

A
- Laterally rotate the shoulder (g/h joint)
- Adduct the shoulder (g/h joint)
- Extend the shoulder (g/h joint)
- Horizontally abduct the shoulder (g/h joint)
- Stabilize head of humerus in glenoid cavity

O Infraspinous fossa of scapula

I Greater tubercle of humerus

N Suprascapular

Infraspinatus

Teres Minor

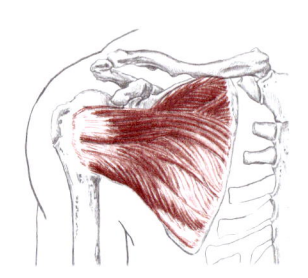

A
- Laterally rotate the shoulder (g/h joint)
- Adduct the shoulder (g/h joint)
- Extend the shoulder (g/h joint)
- Horizontally abduct the shoulder (g/h joint)
- Stabilize head of humerus in glenoid cavity

O Superior half of lateral border of scapula

I Greater tubercle of humerus

N Axillary

Teres minor

Subscapularis

A
- Medially rotate the shoulder (g/h joint)
- Stabilize head of humerus in glenoid cavity

O Subscapular fossa of the scapula

I Lesser tubercle of the humerus

N Upper and lower subscapular

Subscapularis

| TGB, 3rd p. 82-89 | Backpack Shoulder & Arm | Handbook p. 41-42 | DVD Shoulder & Arm |

32 Instructor's Field Guide

Rotator Cuff Muscles

Starter Questions
- Which muscle must you palpate through in order to reach the supraspinatus? *(trapezius)*
- How could you remember the differences between the teres minor and major?
- Which muscle has similar actions to the infraspinatus? *(teres minor)*
- Has anyone received bodywork on their subscapularis? What would be some of the challenges to accessing this muscle?

ADL - Supraspinatus
- Raising a hand to ask a question
- Installing an overhead lightbulb

ADL - Infraspinatus/Teres Minor
- Starting a lawnmower
- Fanning a smoke-filled room wildly with your arms and hands

ADL - Subscapularis
- Scratching your back
- Clutching *Trail Guide to the Body* to your chest

Two Cents

Supraspinatus
- Things become sketchy for students as the muscle belly passes under the acromion.
- Students may not be able to discern the tendon on the greater tubercle. It's a flat tendon lying on a flat portion of bone.

Infraspinatus and Teres Minor
- The trapezius and deltoid cover a good portion of the infraspinatus.
- The "hamburger squeeze" is a great way to find the teres minor. It is the same technique for locating the teres major, but just that much further up into the axilla.

Subscapularis
- A clear demonstration before students palpate can be helpful to set the proper tempo and techniques for accessing this muscle.
- Chances are that most students haven't had their axilla palpated before or explored this region on a partner. So consider having an open dialogue with students about their thoughts and feelings around palpating (and being palpated) in the axilla.
- Gently assure students that this muscle (which looks completely inaccessible) is, with the correct positioning, quite palpable.

Rhomboids

A
- Adduct the scapula (scapulothoracic joint)
- Elevate the scapula (s/t joint)
- Downwardly rotate the scapula (s/t joint)

O *Major:* Spinous processes of T-2 to T-5
Minor: Spinous processes of C-7 and T-1

I *Major:* Medial border of the scapula between spine of the scapula and inferior angle
Minor: Upper portion of medial border of the scapula, across from spine of scapula

N Dorsal scapular from brachial plexus

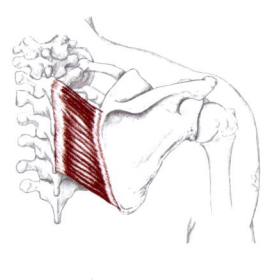

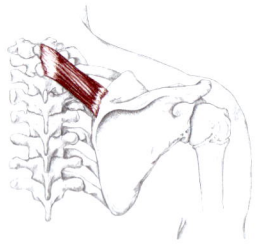

Starter Questions
- Can you name a daily activity that requires your rhomboids?
- Which jobs would likely create strained rhomboids?
  (computer use, house painting, professional cycling and rowing)
- What muscle must you palpate through in order to reach the rhomboids? *(trapezius)*
- What muscles are deep to the rhomboids? *(serratus posterior superior, erector spinae group, intercostals)*

ADL
- Rowing a boat
- Sticking one's chest out, pressing the scapulae together
- Shrugging your shoulders
- Squeezing through a small cave (it could happen on a daily basis)

Two Cents
- Keep in mind that students may not yet be familiar with the spinous processes of the vertebrae.
- The rhomboids are a fine opportunity for students to compare the different fiber directions of surrounding muscles.
- Students may need a little encouragement and instruction to properly mobilize the scapula (via the arm).

TGB, 3rd p. 90-91	Backpack Shoulder & Arm	Handbook p. 43-44	DVD Shoulder & Arm

Levator Scapula

A *Unilaterally:*
- Elevate the scapula (scapulothoracic joint)
- Downwardly rotate the scapula (s/t joint)
- Laterally flex the head and neck
- Rotate the head and neck to the same side

Bilaterally:
- Extend the head and neck

O Transverse processes of first through fourth cervical vertebrae

I Upper region of medial border and superior angle of scapula

N Dorsal scapular and cervical nerves

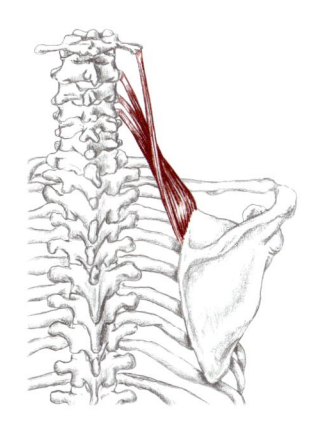

Starter Questions
- The levator performs similar actions with what other muscles that we've learned? *(trapezius and rhomboids)*
- How would the following professionals use their levator scapulae:
    Administrative assistant? *(holding phone between shoulder and ear, forward head posture while viewing a computer)*
    House painters? *(extension of neck and head looking at a ceiling)*

ADL
- Turning head when changing lanes in traffic
- Shrugging shoulders
- Tilting your head to the side because you don't understand an instructor's question

Two Cents
- The "crunchiness" or thickness often felt at the insertion site of the levator scapula is a site of crepitus (a palpatory sensation due to gas in subcutaneous tissues), calcific deposits or scar tissue.
- Consider leading students through a short exercise to locate the cervical TVPs.
- The 3-D aspect of this muscle is a bit confusing. So think about drawing the levator on a shirtless model. This works great to help visualize how it is both on the posterior *and* lateral sides of the neck. (If the model moves his head in various positions, students really see how the muscle shortens and lengthens.)

TGB, 3rd p. 91-93	Backpack Shoulder & Arm	Handbook p. 43-44	DVD Shoulder & Arm

Shoulder & Arm

Serratus Anterior

A *With the origin fixed:*
- Abduct the scapula (scapulothoracic joint)
- Depress the scapula (s/t joint)
- Hold the medial border of scapula against the rib cage

If scapula is fixed:
- May act in forced inhalation

O Surfaces of upper eight or nine ribs

I Anterior surface of medial border of scapula

N Long thoracic

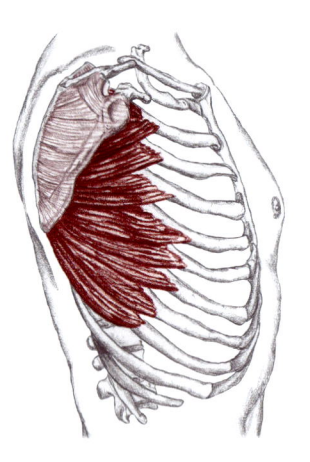

Starter Questions
- What muscle does the serratus anterior "interdigitate" with, creating the ripple effect on the anterior/lateral thorax? *(external oblique)*
- What two muscles lie superficial to the serratus? *(pectoralis major and latissimus dorsi)*
- Given the location of the serratus, do you have any ideas how you could access it? What positions? What actions to contract it?

ADL
- A push-up
- Throwing a punch
- Pushing open a swinging door

Two Cents
- The serratus can be perplexing and frustrating for students. It has thin, deep fibers, it's tucked against the ribs and, when it contracts, there's not much to feel. Students may ask, "Why do we have to learn this muscle?" Well, it plays an important role in respiration, can be involved in a "winged scapula," affects the placement of the scapula on the shoulder and, lastly, responds well to bodywork. Other than that - sure, skip it.

TGB, 3rd p. 94-96	Backpack Shoulder & Arm	Handbook p. 43-44

Pectoralis Major

A *All fibers:*
- Adduct the shoulder (glenohumeral joint)
- Medially rotate the shoulder (g/h joint)
- Assist in elevating the thorax in forced inhalation (if arm is fixed)

Upper fibers:
- Flex the shoulder (g/h joint)
- Horizontally adduct the shoulder

Lower fibers:
- Extend the shoulder (g/h joint)

O Medial half of clavicle, sternum and cartilage of ribs one through six

I Crest of greater tubercle of humerus

N Medial and lateral pectoral

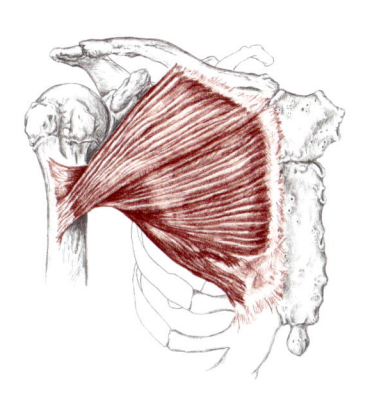

Starter Questions
- How many bones does the pectoralis major attach to? *(three bones - sternum, clavicle and humerus, plus the cartilage of ribs 1 - 6)*
- What sports would require strong pecs? *(arm wrestling, pitching, swimming and chin-ups)*
- How would you passively shorten the upper fibers of the pectoralis major? *(flex and horizontally adduct the shoulder)*

ADL
- Doing a chin-up
- Almost every swim stroke ever invented
- Sawing a piece of wood (both directions)

Two Cents
- Accessing the serratus and the pectorals means palpating around breast tissue. Expect that students will see this palpatory intersection long before the actual class. So what can you do to steer them in the right direction? Assign the boxes on pages 95 and 98 in *Trail Guide* as essential reading for students.
- Remind students that men have mammary tissue as well - just not as much.

TGB, 3rd p. 97-99	Backpack Shoulder & Arm	Handbook p. 43-44	DVD Shoulder & Arm

Shoulder & Arm 37

Pectoralis Minor

A
- Depress the scapula (scapulothoracic joint)
- Abduct the scapula (s/t joint)
- Tilt the scapula anteriorly (s/t joint)
- Assist in forced inhalation (if scapula is fixed)

O Third, fourth and fifth ribs

I Coracoid process of scapula

N Medial pectoral

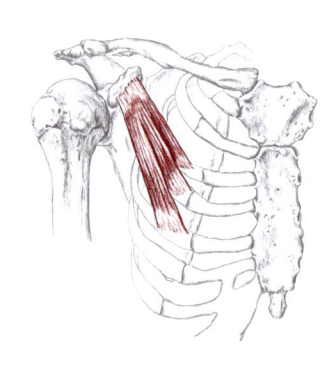

Starter Questions
- Regarding how they position the scapula, can you see any connection between the pectoralis minor and the rhomboids? *(pec minor - depress and abduct; rhomboids - elevate and adduct)*
- What nerve plexus and artery pass deep to the pectoralis minor? *(brachial plexus and axillary artery)*
- What can you do to ensure that the vessels coursing deep to the pectoralis minor will be unimpaired while you explore this muscle? *(palpate slowly, check in with your partner)*

ADL
- Throwing a punch
- Reaching into a deep front pocket
- Forced inhalation

Two Cents
- Since the pectoralis minor can be challenging for students to palpate, remind them of **p**ositioning, hand **p**lacement and **p**atience (go slowly).
- When palpating through the pectoralis major, the coracoid process is an easy place to begin.
- This is a great muscle to draw out on one side of the body and then palpate on the other side.

TGB, 3rd p.100-101	Backpack Shoulder & Arm	Handbook p. 43-44

38 Instructor's Field Guide

Biceps Brachii

A
- Flex the elbow (humeroulnar joint)
- Supinate the forearm (radioulnar joints)
- Flex the shoulder (glenohumeral joint)

O *Short head:*
   Coracoid process of scapula
Long head:
   Supraglenoid tubercle of scapula

I Tuberosity of the radius and aponeurosis of the biceps brachii

N Musculocutaneous

Starter Questions
- Which muscle is the strongest supinator of the forearm? *(biceps brachii)*
- The biceps is partially deep to which two muscles? *(deltoid and pectoralis major)*
- How could you position the elbow and forearm to passively shorten the biceps brachii? *(flex the elbow and supinate the forearm)*

ADL
- Holding a heavy hymn book while singing in the church choir
- With your right arm, using a screwdriver to tighten a screw
- Carrying an infant in your arms in a cradled position

Two Cents
- Since students are usually already familiar with the biceps' name and general location, this can be a fun muscle to explore.
- Palpation of the belly comes easily, but the proximal and distal ends are more challenging.
- Students will also ask if the two heads of the biceps can be distinguished separately. Generally not. In the most proximal aspects, as the belly tucks under the deltoid, you can sometimes feel the belly separating into two distinct halves.

TGB, 3rd p. 103-104	Backpack Shoulder & Arm	Handbook p. 45-46	DVD Shoulder & Arm

Shoulder & Arm

Triceps Brachii

A *All heads:*
  - Extend the elbow (humeroulnar joint)
  Long head:
  - Extend the shoulder (glenohumeral joint)
  - Adduct the shoulder (g/h joint)

O *Long head:*
    Infraglenoid tubercle of scapula
  Lateral head:
    Posterior surface of proximal half of humerus
  Medial head:
    Posterior surface of distal half of humerus

I Olecranon process of ulna

N Radial

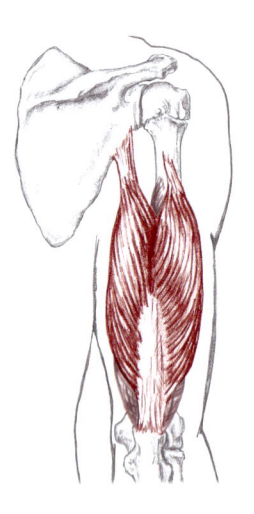

Starter Questions
- Why do you think the triceps has three heads instead of just one? *(As the sole extensor of the elbow, the triceps requires a sizeable area to attach. But where? Unlike the broad origin sites of the pec major or latissimus dorsi, the triceps has little surface area from which to originate. So by dividing itself into three bellies, it maximizes the posterior surfaces of the humerus, but also functions properly.)*
- What do you irritate when you "hit your funny bone?" *(ulnar nerve, which runs medial to the triceps tendon and olecranon process at the elbow)*
- The long head of the triceps weaves between which two shoulder muscles? *(teres major and teres minor)*

ADL
- Slamming the trunk of a car
- Pounding in large nails with a big ol' hammer
- Raising your body during the up phase of a push-up

Two Cents
- If students become perplexed by the triceps, gently guide them back to the olecranon process. This prominent landmark is the best starting point for them to progress proximally, defining the triceps' edges and feeling its central tendon.

TGB, 3rd p. 105-106	Backpack Shoulder & Arm	Handbook p. 45-46	DVD Shoulder & Arm

Coracobrachialis

A
- Flex the shoulder (glenohumeral joint)
- Adduct the shoulder (g/h joint)

O Coracoid process of scapula

I Medial surface of mid-humeral shaft

N Musculocutaneous

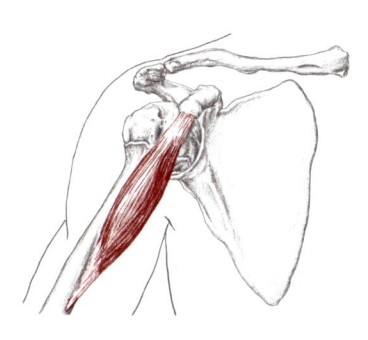

Starter Questions
- How many muscles attach to the coracoid process? *(three - coracobrachialis, short head of biceps brachii, pectoralis minor)*
- How can you position the arm to best access this muscle? *(laterally rotate and abduct the shoulder to 45°)*
- How many muscles adduct the shoulder? *(seven - coracobrachialis, pec major, latissimus dorsi, teres major, teres minor, infraspinatus, triceps brachii)*

ADL
- Reaching around your face to scratch your opposite ear
- Doing a bench press when weightlifting
- A martial arts forearm block in front of the chest

Two Cents
- Although the coracobrachialis can be an elusive muscle to access, most of the difficulties disappear with proper positioning of the shoulder - laterally rotated and abducted.

TGB, 3rd p. 107	Backpack Shoulder & Arm	Handbook p. 45-46

Other Structures

	TGB, 3rd ed.
Axilla	108
Sternoclavicular Joint	109
Ligaments of the Shoulder	110
Glenohumeral Joint	110
Coracoclavicular Ligament	112
Coracoacromial Ligament	112
Subacromial Bursa	113
Axillary Lymph Nodes	113
Brachial Artery	114

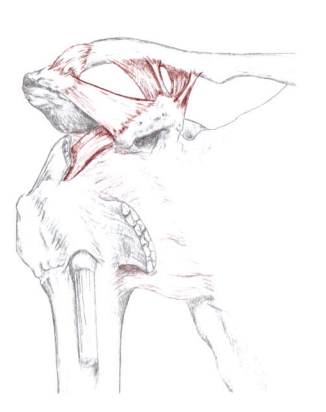

TGB, 3rd p. 108-114	Backpack Shoulder & Arm	Handbook p. 47-50

42   Instructor's Field Guide

NOTES

3 Forearm & Hand

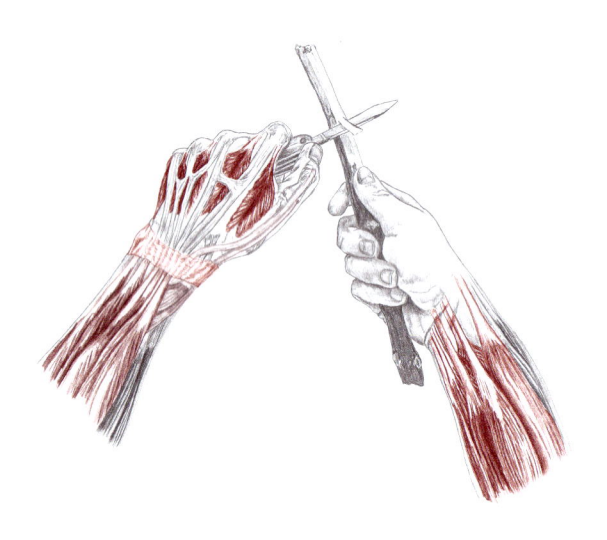

Topography	45
Skin & Fascia	45
Bones	45
Bony Landmark Trails	46-47
Muscles	48-61
Other Structures	62

Topography

| TGB, 3rd p. 116 | Handbook p. 52 |

Skin & Fascia

| TGB, 3rd p. 117 |

Bones

| TGB, 3rd p. 118-120 | Handbook p. 53-58 |

Starter Questions

- How many carpal bones are there? *(eight)*
- What two bones comprise the forearm? *(radius and ulna)*
- Where is the "arm" and where is the "forearm?" *(arm - shoulder to elbow; forearm - elbow to wrist)*

Two Cents

- Engage students in writing and speaking the long, intimidating joint names of the forearm, wrist and hand. In class you could ask them to say these names frequently. For example, "Turn to your classmate and tell them what a lovely *radioulnar* joint they have." (This way they're not put "on the spot.")
- Emphasize to students that palpatory knowledge of the bony landmarks of the forearm will smooth the path to locating the long, slender muscles of the forearm.

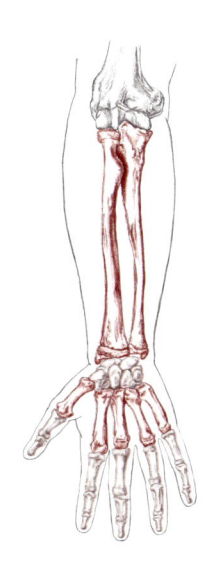

Forearm & Hand 45

Bony Landmark Trails

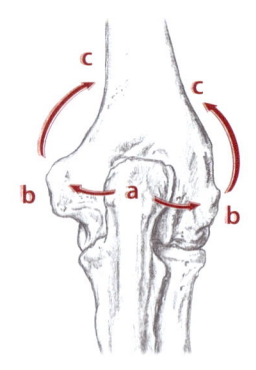

Trail 1 "Knob Hill" explores the elbow and distal humerus.

- **a** Olecranon process and fossa
- **b** Epicondyles of humerus
- **c** Supracondylar ridges of humerus

Trail 2 "The Razor's Edge" follows the length of the superficial ulna.

- **a** Olecranon process
- **b** Shaft of the ulna
- **c** Head of the ulna
- **d** Styloid process of the ulna

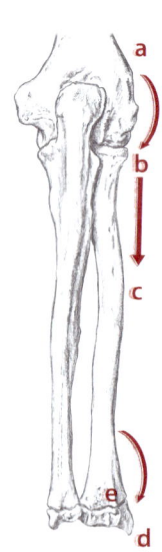

Trail 3 "Pivot Pass" travels the length of the radius, the bone that creates the pivoting action of the forearm.

- **a** Lateral epicondyle of the humerus
- **b** Head of the radius
- **c** Shaft of the radius
- **d** Styloid process of the radius
- **e** Lister's tubercle

Trail 4 "Walking On Your Hands" explores the small carpal bones of the wrist as well as the bones and joints of the hand.

TGB, 3rd
p. 121-134

Bony Landmark Trails

Two Cents
- Something you might want to ask yourself: "How experienced and confident am I palpating the carpals?" As mentioned before, we teach to our strengths and our weaknesses. Maybe you were never taught how to access the carpals. If you are not confident exploring these bones, chances are your students won't be either. Consider reviewing the carpals with a more experienced instructor or reviewing this information in *Trail Guide*.
- Emphasize that there are four sides from which to access the carpals. Knowing the options can make the explorative process much easier.
- Begin teaching the easier aspects, such as the carpals as a group and the pisiform, and then progress to the more challenging material.
- Ease students' potential frustrations by acknowledging that this is a region of the body that takes practice and patience.

Muscles of the Forearm & Hand

	Field Guide	**TGB, 3rd ed.**
Anconeus	53	147
Brachialis	49	140
Brachioradialis	50	141
Extensors of the Wrist and Hand	51	143
Flexors of the Wrist and Hand	54	148
Long Muscles of the Thumb	60	157
Pronator Quadratus	57	155
Pronator Teres	57	154
Short Muscles of the Thumb	59	157
Supinator	58	155

Starter Questions

- The muscles of the elbow, forearm and hand can be arranged into four groups. What are they? *(see p. 135 in Trail Guide)*
- Can you name a muscle that creates more than one action at the wrist? *(see p. 133 in Field Guide for list of muscles that effect the wrist)*
- "Flexor carpi ulnaris" - what information can you gather about this muscle from its name?
    - *it's a flexor*
    - *there must be an extensor carpi ulnaris*
    - *it flexes the carpals (crosses the wrist joint)*
    - *there's a muscle that flexes the digits*
    - *it's on the ulnar side of forearm*

TGB, 3rd p. 135-139	Backpack Forearm & Hand	Handbook p. 59-68	DVD Forearm & Hand

Instructor's Field Guide

Brachialis

A Flex the elbow (humeroulnar joint)

O Distal half of anterior surface of humerus

I Tuberosity and coronoid process of ulna

N Musculocutaneous

Starter Questions
- Can you name a synergist to the brachialis? *(biceps brachii, brachioradialis, most of the flexors, pronator teres)*
- What is a bony landmark that can help you locate the brachialis? *(deltoid tuberosity)*
- What are two vessels that pass along the medial side of the brachialis? *(brachial artery and median nerve)*

ADL
- Bringing food from the plate to your mouth
- Carrying a load of anatomy books
- Pumping your fists in the air after you win public office

Two Cents
- The brachialis can be a deceptively challenging muscle for students to get a handle on. First of all, it may be difficult to visualize its location and shape on the arm. You can make it easier for students by bringing their attention first to the lateral edge of the brachialis belly.
- If you've taught students the biceps brachii already, take advantage of this knowledge. Sometimes isolating the biceps can make the process much easier for students. You can tell them: "If all of this tissue is the biceps," as you grasp the belly, "then everything deep to it is the brachialis."
- Ask a physically well-developed student to flex his elbow to 90° and tighten his arm. Oftentimes you can clearly define the edge of the biceps enough to see the deeper brachialis.

TGB, 3rd p. 140	Backpack Forearm & Hand	Handbook p. 69-70	DVD Forearm & Hand

Forearm & Hand

Brachioradialis

A
- Flex the elbow (humeroulnar joint)
- Assist to pronate and supinate the forearm when these movements are resisted

O Lateral supracondylar ridge of humerus

I Styloid process of radius

N Radial

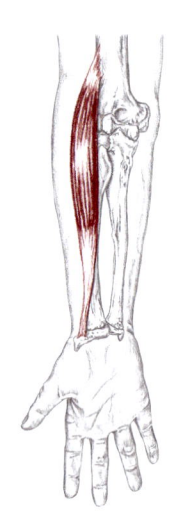

Starter Questions
- How many muscles supinate the forearm and what are they?
  (Three: biceps brachii, supinator, brachioradialis)
- This muscle serves as a dividing line between which two muscle groups?
  (flexors and extensors of the wrist and hand)
- Which joint(s) does this muscle cross? *(humeroulnar/humeroradial - the elbow, but not the radiocarpal - the wrist)*

ADL
- Turning a door handle or screwdriver
- Combing your hair
- Bringing a beer stein up to one's mouth

Two Cents
- This is often a fun muscle for students to explore - highly visible and palpable.
- Acknowledge for students that the distal half of the belly is far less distinguishable than the bulkier, proximal portion.
- Consider starting students at the radial tuberosity and sliding proximally to feel the flat tendon enlarge into the belly.

TGB, 3rd p. 141	Backpack Forearm & Hand	Handbook p. 69-70	DVD Forearm & Hand

Extensors of the Wrist and Hand

Extensor Carpi Radialis Longus & Brevis

A
- Extend the wrist (radiocarpal joint)
- Abduct the wrist (radiocarpal joint)
- Assist to flex the elbow (humeroulnar joint)

O Lateral supracondylar ridge of humerus

I *Longus:* Base of second metacarpal
Brevis: Base of third metacarpal

N Radial

Radialis longus    Radialis brevis

Extensor Carpi Ulnaris

A
- Extend the wrist (radiocarpal joint)
- Adduct the wrist (radiocarpal joint)

O Common extensor tendon from lateral epicondyle of humerus

I Base of fifth metacarpal

N Radial

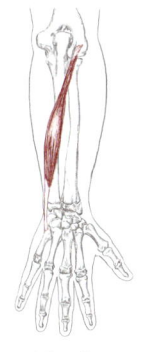

Ulnaris

Extensor Digitorum

A
- Extend the second through fifth fingers (metacarpophalangeal and interphalangeal joints)
- Assist to extend the wrist (radiocarpal joint)

O Common extensor tendon from the lateral epicondyle of humerus

I Middle and distal phalanges of second through fifth fingers

N Radial

Digitorum

TGB, 3rd p. 143-146	Backpack Forearm & Hand	Handbook p. 71-72	DVD Forearm & Hand

Forearm & Hand

Extensors of the Wrist and Hand

Starter Questions/All Extensors
- Which of these four muscles is located alongside the shaft of the ulna? *(extensor carpi ulnaris)*
- Which of these muscles are antagonists? And for which actions? *(extensor carpi radialis longus and brevis - abduct the wrist; extensor carpi ulnaris - adduct the wrist)*
- Can you name a bony landmark that would help you locate one of these muscles?

ADL/Radialis
- Stabilizing the wrist during gripping, like opening a jar
- Scrubbing a dirty plate

ADL/Digitorum
- Playing the piano or trumpet
- Holding your hand up while giving the Vulcan hand greeting (the wrist part, not the finger part)

ADL/Ulnaris
- Shaping clay
- During massage when fanning the wrist into ulnar deviation at the end of a gliding stroke

---

Two Cents
- The extensors are positioned side-by-side; the flexors are positioned in layers.
- Be methodical. When reciting the names of these muscles, use the same order and encourage the students to say the names of these muscles in class.
- Try introducing and palpating the extensor carpi radialis longus and brevis together. Also, prepare students for the fact that the distal, tendinous four inches of these muscles seem to disappear along the shaft of the radius.
- Also, for the extensor carpi radialis muscles: When their partners abduct their wrist, point out for students that this action can't possibly be created by the brachioradialis because that muscle doesn't cross the wrist joint.
- If you have a student with sinewy or well-developed forearms, ask him to hold his forearm up (palm toward his face) and slowly wiggle his fingers at the metacarpophalangeal joints. This position will display the undulating portions of the extensor digitorum.

Anconeus

A Extend the elbow (humeroulnar joint)

O Lateral epicondyle of the humerus

I Olecranon process and lateral edge of ulnar shaft

N Radial nerve

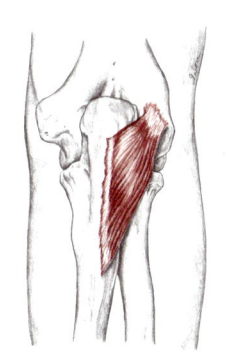

Starter Question
- What three bony landmarks could help you isolate the anconeus?
  (lateral epicondyle, olecranon process, edge of ulnar shaft)

ADL
- Assist triceps brachii with board-splitting judo chop

Two Cents
- Since this muscle can be confusing to visualize on the forearm, consider asking a student to assume the "Rosie the Riveter" pose (shoulder and elbow flexed at 90°) and drawing it on the forearm.

| TGB, 3rd p. 147 | Backpack Forearm & Hand |

Forearm & Hand 53

Flexors of the Wrist and Hand

Flexor Carpi Radialis

A
- Flex the wrist (radiocarpal joint)
- Abduct the wrist (radiocarpal joint)
- Flex the elbow (humeroulnar joint)

O Common flexor tendon from medial epicondyle

I Bases of second and third metacarpals

N Median

Radialis

Palmaris Longus

A
- Tense the palmar fascia
- Flex the wrist (radiocarpal joint)
- Flex the elbow (humeroulnar joint)

O Common flexor tendon from medial epicondyle

I Flexor retinaculum and palmar aponeurosis

N Median

Palmaris

Flexor Carpi Ulnaris

A
- Flex the wrist (radiocarpal joint)
- Adduct the wrist (radiocarpal joint)
- Assist to flex the elbow (humeroulnar joint)

O *Humeral head:* Common flexor tendon from medial epicondyle of humerus
Ulnar head: Posterior surface of proximal half of ulnar shaft

I Pisiform

N Ulnar

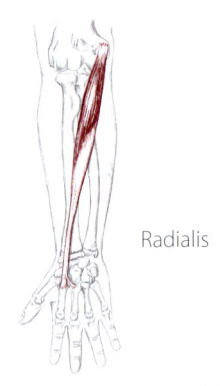

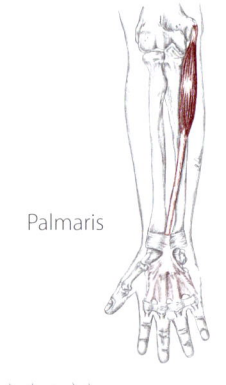

Ulnaris

TGB, 3rd p. 148-153	Backpack Forearm & Hand	Handbook p. 71-72	DVD Forearm & Hand

54 Instructor's Field Guide

Flexors of the Wrist and Hand

Flexor Digitorum Superficialis

A • Flex the second through fifth fingers (metacarpophalangeal and proximal interphalangeal joints)
• Flex the wrist (radiocarpal joint)

O Common flexor tendon from medial epicondyle of humerus, ulnar collateral ligament, coronoid process of ulna and shaft of radius

I By four tendons into sides of middle phalanges of second through fifth fingers

N Ulnar

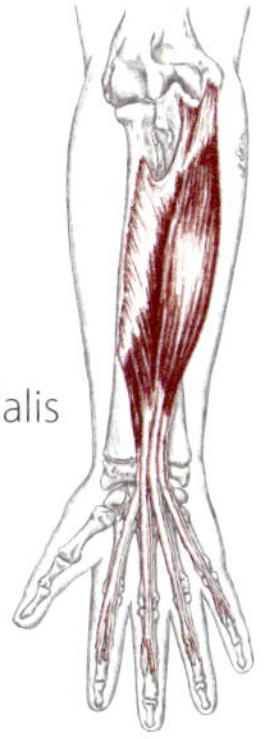

Superficialis

Flexor Digitorum Profundus

A • Flex the second through fifth fingers (metacarpophalangeal and distal interphalangeal joints)
• Assist to flex the wrist (radiocarpal joint)

O Anterior and medial surfaces of proximal three-quarters of ulna

I By four tendons into bases of distal phalanges, palmar surface of second through fifth fingers

N Ulnar

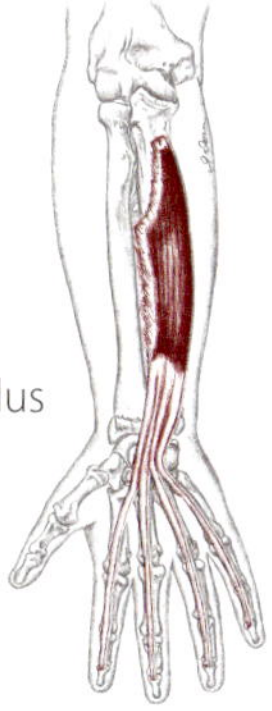

Profundus

Starter Questions/All Flexors

- What are the two structures that divide the flexors from the extensors? *(brachioradialis and the shaft of the ulna)*
- How many flexor layers are there? *(three: superficial, intermediate and deep)*
- Which muscles are superficial? *(flexor carpi radialis, palmaris longus, flexor carpi ulnaris)*
- Which carpal serves as an easy bony landmark to isolate the insertion of the flexor carpi ulnaris? *(pisiform)*

Flexors of the Wrist and Hand

ADL/All Flexors
- Playing guitar
- Making a snowball
- Typing
- Picking up small objects (needles, coins)
- Tying shoelaces
- Holding onto the rail of a fast-moving train
- Hold a cellphone

Two Cents
- These muscles have long names, are squeezed together and have similar actions. So be slow and clear and take it step-by-step.
- The extensors are positioned side-by-side; the flexors are positioned in layers.
- Be methodical. When reciting the names of the muscles, use the same order. Try to identify the muscles from superficial to deep.
- Three short demonstrations (students gathered around, five minutes max) will serve students better than one long demo (too much information, eyes glaze over).
- Astute students will note that the flexor carpi ulnaris, unlike the extensor carpi ulnaris, does not lay exactly next to the ulnar shaft. And they're right! Instead, the belly runs about a half inch away. So the question arises, "What's the muscle tissue that is between the flexor carpi ulnaris and the ulnar shaft?" This is a fine opportunity to mention the flexor digitorum muscles.

Pronator Teres

A
- Pronate the forearm (radioulnar joints)
- Assist to flex the elbow (humeroulnar joint)

O Medial epicondyle of humerus, common flexor tendon and coronoid process of ulna

I Middle of lateral surface of radius

N Median

Pronator Quadratus

A Pronate the forearm (radioulnar joints)

O Medial, anterior surface of distal ulna

I Lateral, anterior surface of distal radius

N Median

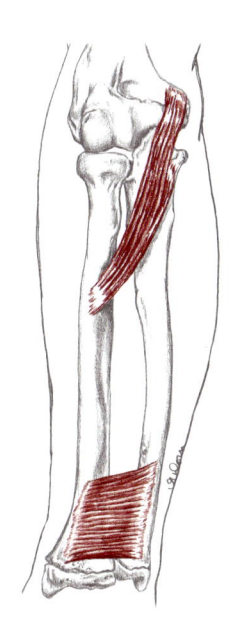

Starter Questions
- During pronation which muscles are antagonists to the pronators? *(biceps brachii, supinator, brachioradialis)*
- How many muscles pronate the forearm? *(three: pronator teres, pronator quadratus and brachioradialis)*
- How could the fiber direction of pronator teres help to discern it from the other superficial flexors? *(its fibers run diagonally along the forearm)*

ADL
- Turning a doorknob
- Unscrewing the lid on a jelly jar (with your right forearm and hand)

Two Cents
- Emphasize the directional difference between the pronator and its neighboring flexors. Also, drawing the muscle on the forearm can be very helpful.
- Encourage students to gently "clunk" their thumbs across the pronator's belly - a most distinguishable "speed bump."
- Pronator quadratus is an advanced palpatory muscle, but certainly worth discussing in respect to its "balancing" qualities for the pronator teres.

TGB, 3rd p. 154, 155	Backpack Forearm & Hand	Handbook p. 69-70	DVD Forearm & Hand

Supinator

A Supinate the forearm (radioulnar joints)

O Radial collateral ligament, annular ligament and supinator crest of ulna

I Lateral surface of proximal shaft of radius

N Radial

Starter Questions
- The supinator is deep to which superficial muscle group? *(the extensors)*
- What muscle serves as the main synergist of the supinator? *(biceps brachii)*
- The supinator is superficial to what bony landmark of the radius? *(the head)*

ADL
- Digging out a big scoop of ice cream
- Swirling the water in a bathtub
- Folding your clothes

Two Cents
- The supinator's attachment sites can be confusing to visualize, so consider drawing it on a model's forearm.
- Due to its buried location, anticipate some impatience from students unable to discern the muscle's belly.
- Exploration of the supinator can sometimes aggravate the radial nerve.

TGB, 3rd	Backpack	Handbook
p. 155-156	Forearm & Hand	p. 69-70

Muscles of the Thumb (short)

Opponens Pollicis

A • Opposition of the thumb at the carpometacarpal joint (bringing the pads of the thumb and fifth finger together)

O Flexor retinaculum and tubercle of the trapezium

I Entire length of first metacarpal bone, radial side

N Median

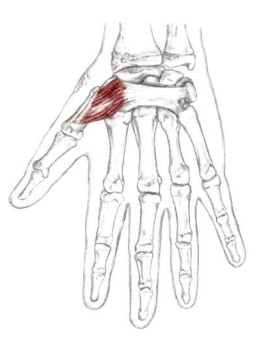

Opponens pollicis

Adductor Pollicis

A • Adduct the thumb (carpometacarpal and metacarpophalangeal joints)
• Assist in flexion of the thumb (metacarpophalangeal joint)

O Capitate, second and third metacarpals

I Base of proximal phalange of thumb

N Ulnar

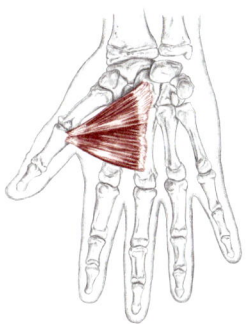

Adductor pollicis

Abductor Pollicis Brevis

A • Abduct the thumb (carpometacarpal, metacarpophalangeal joints)
• Assist in opposition of the thumb

O Flexor retinaculum, trapezium and scaphoid tubercles

I Base of proximal phalange of thumb

N Median

Abductor pollicis brevis

Flexor Pollicis Brevis

A • Flex the thumb (carpometacarpal, metacarpophalangeal joints)
• Assist in opposition of thumb

O *Superficial head:* Flexor retinaculum
Deep head: Trapezium, trapezoid and capitate

I Base of proximal phalange of thumb

N Median and ulnar

Flexor pollicis brevis

Forearm & Hand

Muscles of the Thumb (long)

Abductor Pollicis Longus

A • Abduct the thumb (carpometacarpal joint)
  • Extend the thumb (carpometacarpal joint)

O Posterior surface of radius and ulna and interosseous membrane

I Base of first metacarpal

N Radial

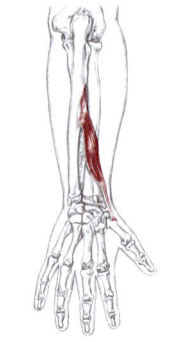

Abductor pollicis longus

Extensor Pollicis Longus and Brevis

A • Extend the thumb (interphalangeal joint)
  • Assist to extend the thumb (metacarpophalangeal, carpometacarpal joints)

O *Longus:* Posterior surface of ulna and interosseous membrane
  Brevis: Posterior surface of radius and interosseous membrane

I *Longus:* Distal phalange of thumb
  Brevis: Proximal phalange of thumb

N Radial

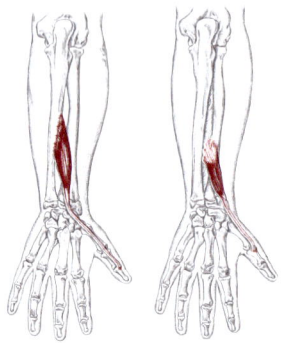

Extensor pollicis l. & b.

Flexor Pollicis Longus

A • Flex the thumb (interphalangeal joint)
  • Assist to flex the thumb (metacarpophalangeal, carpometacarpal joints)

O Anterior surface of radius and interosseous membrane

I Distal phalange of thumb

N Median

Flexor pollicis longus

TGB, 3rd p. 157-162	Backpack Forearm & Hand	Handbook p. 73-74	DVD Forearm & Hand

Instructor's Field Guide

Muscles of the Thumb

Starter Questions
- The thumb muscles can be divided into which two groups? *(short and long muscles)*
- How many short muscles are there? *(four)* Long muscles? *(four)*
- What is the proper name for the pad of the thumb? *(thenar eminence)*
- Why do you think the body assigned eight different muscles to move the thumb?

ADL/Muscles of the Thumb
- Hitchhiking
- Sewing
- Writing
- Painting
- Squeezing a fruit
- Throwing a ball

ADL/Opponens Pollicis
- Holding a pencil
- Grasping the handle of a teacup
- Unlocking a door with a key

Two Cents
- Like the flexors and extensors, the names of the thumb muscles can be immensely confusing. Try creating structure for students by putting these muscles into groups: short, long, flexors, extensors, etc.
- Many of the thumb muscles do not have discernible attachment sites. This can be discouraging for students. Be honest with students right from the start that these are challenging muscles to isolate.
- Using the white board, draw a circle, divide it into four sections and add a circle in the center. Label the sections (below) and then put the thumb muscles in the appropriate area(s). Muscles that perform two actions will fall between two sections.

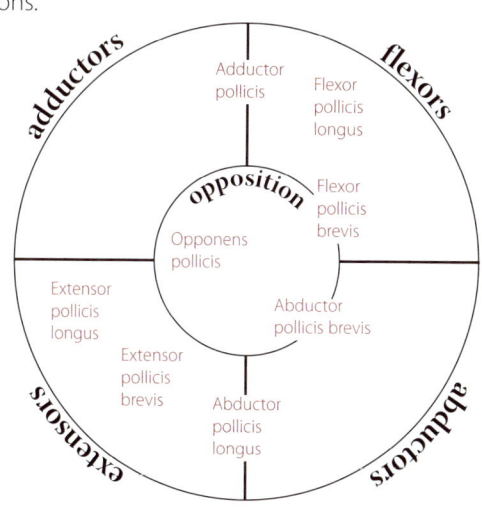

Diagram: Circle divided into four quadrants labeled adductors, flexors, abductors, extensors, *with* opposition *in the center circle.*

- Adductor pollicis (adductors)
- Flexor pollicis longus (flexors)
- Flexor pollicis brevis (flexors)
- Abductor pollicis brevis (abductors)
- Abductor pollicis longus (abductors)
- Extensor pollicis brevis (extensors)
- Extensor pollicis longus (extensors)
- Opponens pollicis (opposition)

Forearm & Hand

Other Structures

	TGB, 3rd ed.
Radial Collateral Ligament	166
Ulnar Collateral Ligament	167
Annular Ligament	167
Ulnar Nerve	167
Olecranon Bursa	168
Interosseous Membrane	168
Retinacula of the Wrist	169
Palmar Aponeurosis	169
Radial and Ulnar Arteries	170
Ligaments of the Wrist and Hand	171

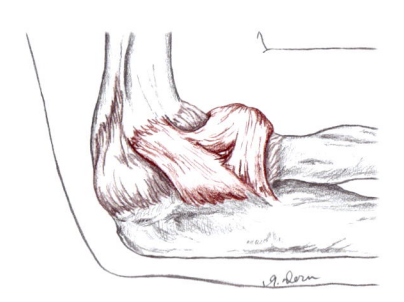

TGB, 3rd	Backpack	Handbook
p. 166-172	Forearm & Hand	p. 75-78

NOTES

4 Spine & Thorax

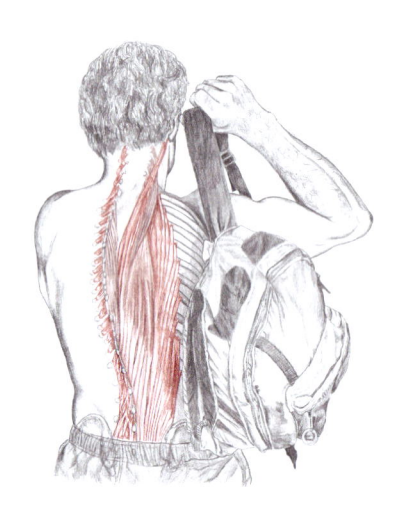

Topography	65
Skin & Fascia	65
Bones	65
Bony Landmark Trails	66-67
Muscles	68-80
Other Structures	81

Topography

| TGB, 3rd p.174 | Handbook p. 80 |

Skin & Fascia

| TGB, 3rd p. 175 |

Bones

| TGB, 3rd p. 176-179 | Handbook p. 81-87 |

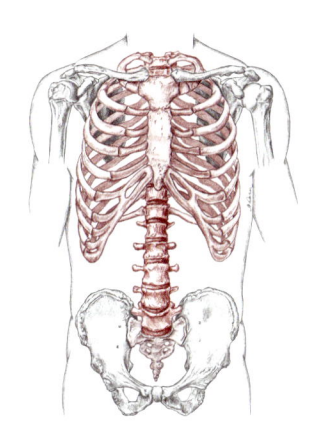

Starter Questions
- How many cervical, thoracic and lumbar vertebrae are there? *(seven, twelve, five)*
- Which vertebral section has the greatest range of motion? *(cervical)*
- All of the vertebrae have common bony landmarks. What are they? *(a body, a vertebral foramen, facets, lamina grooves, transverse processes, and a spinous process - except C-1)*

Spine & Thorax 65

Bony Landmark Trails

Trail 1 "Midline Ridge" explores the spinous processes of the vertebrae and the spaces between them as they run down the middle of the back.

Trail 2 "Crossing Paths" describes surrounding bony landmarks that intersect with specific spinous processes.

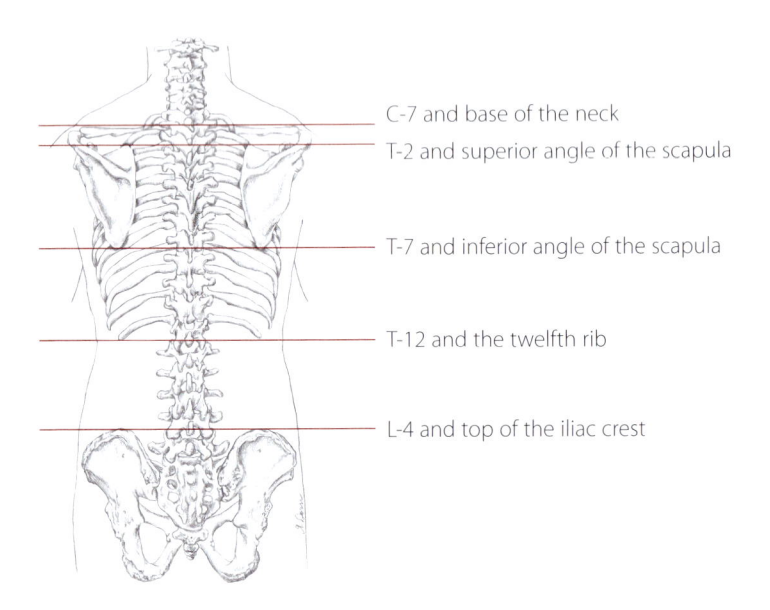

- C-7 and base of the neck
- T-2 and superior angle of the scapula
- T-7 and inferior angle of the scapula
- T-12 and the twelfth rib
- L-4 and top of the iliac crest

Trail 3 "Nape Lane" locates the landmarks of the cervical vertebrae.

- a Spinous processes of the cervicals
- b Transverse processes of the cervicals
- c Lamina groove of the cervicals

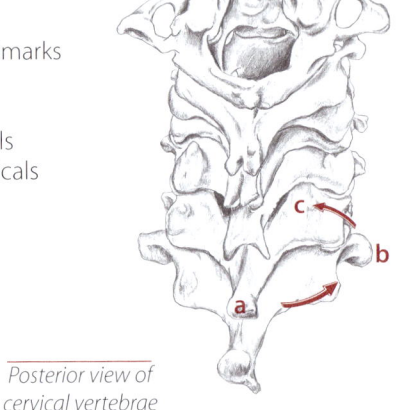

Posterior view of cervical vertebrae

66 **Instructor's Field Guide**

Erector Spinae Group

Erector Spinae Group

A *Unilaterally:*
- Laterally flex vertebral column to the same side

Bilaterally:
- Extend the vertebral column

O Common tendon (thoracolumbar aponeurosis) that attaches to the posterior surface of sacrum, iliac crest, spinous processes of the lumbar and last two thoracic vertebrae

I Various attachments at the posterior ribs, spinous and transverse processes of thoracic and cervical vertebrae, and mastoid process of temporal bone

N Dorsal primary divisions of spinal nerves

❋ ❋ ❋

Branches of the Erector Spinae Group

Spinalis

O Spinous processes of the upper lumbar and lower thoracic vertebrae **(thoracis)**
Ligamentum nuchae, spinous process of C-7 **(cervicis)**

I Spinous processes of upper thoracic **(thoracis)**
Spinous processes of cervicals, except C-1 **(cervicis)**

❋ ❋ ❋

Longissimus

O Common tendon **(thoracis)**
Transverse processes of upper five thoracic vertebrae **(cervicis and capitis)**

I Lower nine ribs and transverse processes of thoracic vertebrae **(thoracis)**
Transverse processes of cervical vertebrae **(cervicis)**
Mastoid process of temporal bone **(capitis)**

❋ ❋ ❋

Iliocostalis

O Common tendon **(lumborum)**
Posterior surface of ribs 1-12 **(thoracis and cervicis)**

I Transverse processes of lumbar vertebrae 1-3 and posterior surface of ribs 6-12 **(lumborum)**
Posterior surface of ribs 1-6 **(thoracis)**
Transverse processes of lower cervicals **(cervicis)**

Spinalis

Longissimus

Iliocostalis

Spine & Thorax

Erector Spinae Group

Starter Questions
- What is the most lateral branch of the erector spinae? *(iliocostalis)*
- What is an everyday activity that would require your erector spinae muscles to lengthen?
- What are two muscles you need to palpate through to access the erectors? *(latissimus dorsi, trapezius, rhomboids, serratus posterior superior and inferior)*

ADL
- Maintaining an upright posture
- Returning to anatomical position after tying your shoes
- Picking up a heavy suitcase (lateral flexion)

Two Cents
- Even though they're large and long, the interwoven and layered arrangement of the erectors can create confusion for students. Consider relieving their anxiety by guiding them to these muscles as a group and later isolating them individually.
- This is a fine set of muscles for students to write and draw the muscles' names and attachment sites on blank skeleton pages (see Spine & Thorax section in the *Field Guide Backpack*).
- Consider having students explore the erectors while their standing partners slowly flex and extend their vertebral columns.

> The upper fibers of longissimus and iliocostalis muscles (longissimus cervicis and capitis, iliocostalis cervicis) assist in extension, lateral flexion and rotation of the head and neck to the same side.

Erector Spinae

TGB, 3rd p. 202-205	Backpack Spine & Thorax	Handbook p. 102-103	DVD Spine & Thorax

Transversospinalis

TGB, 3rd p. 206-208	Backpack Spine & Thorax	Handbook p. 102-103

Transversospinalis Group

Multifidi and Rotatores

A *Unilaterally:* Rotate the vertebral column to the opposite side

Bilaterally: Extend the vertebral column

O *Multifidi:*
Sacrum and transverse processes of lumbar through cervical vertebrae

Rotatores:
Transverse processes of lumbar through cervical vertebrae

I Spinous processes of lumbar vertebrae through second cervical vertebra
(Multifidi span 2-4 vertebrae; rotatores span 1-2)

N Dorsal primary divisions of spinal nerves

❊ ❊ ❊

Semispinalis Capitis

A Extend the vertebral column and head

O Transverse processes of thoracic vertebrae, articular processes of lower cervicals

I Spinous processes of upper thoracic and cervicals (except C-1), and superior nuchal line of occiput

N Dorsal primary divisions of spinal nerves

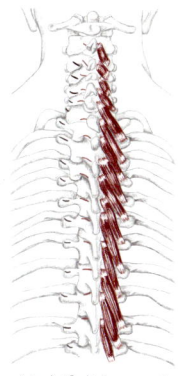

Multifidi (upper)

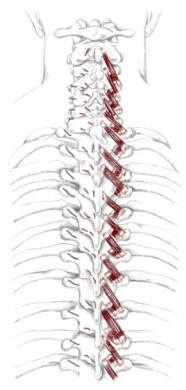

Rotatores (upper)

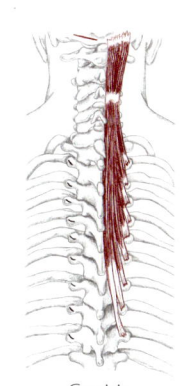

Capitis

Starter Questions
- What are the three branches of the transversospinalis group? *(multifidi, rotatores, semispinalis capitis)*
- The multifidi span how many vertebrae? *(2-4)*
  How many do the rotatores span? *(1-2)*
- These muscles can be found between which two bony landmarks of the spine? *(TVPs and SPs)*

ADL
- Rotating your body's trunk to strap on a seat belt
- Arching and rotating your spine for one of those big "power yawns"

Two Cents
- Oftentimes students will have their hands in the right location but complain of "not feeling anything." Reassure them that this is a good start and with practice and patience these muscles will become more discernible.

Spine & Thorax

Splenius Capitis and Cervicis

A *Unilaterally:*
- Rotate the head and neck to the same side
- Laterally flex the head and neck

Bilaterally:
- Extend the head and neck

O *Capitis:* Ligamentum nuchae, spinous processes of C-7 to T-3
Cervicis: Spinous processes of T-3 to T-6

I *Capitis:* Mastoid process, lateral portion of superior nuchal line
Cervicis: Transverse processes of the upper cervical vertebrae

N Branches of dorsal division of cervical

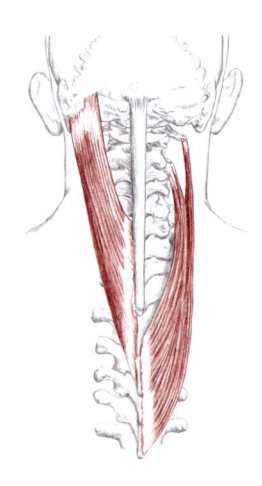

Capitis   Cervicis

Starter Questions
- What muscle is just anterior to the splenius capitis on the lateral neck? *(levator scapula)*
- How is the fiber direction of the splenius capitis different than other spine muscles? *(they run at an oblique angle)*

ADL
- Rotating your head and neck before changing lanes in traffic
- Applying ear drops (holding your head in lateral flexion)
- Crouched over in a huddle during a football game (holding your head up in extension)

Two Cents
- Students might assume that these muscles can be accessed only from a prone position. Yet, supine position offers terrific possibilities.
- Emphasizing the capitis' superficial portion and its oblique fiber direction can help differentiate it from surrounding cervical muscles.
- With their partner supine, ask a student to passively rotate their partner's head from side to side and verbally state if the left (or right) splenii are shortening or lengthening.

TGB, 3rd p. 209-210	Backpack Spine & Thorax	Handbook p. 104-105	DVD Spine & Thorax

Suboccipitals

All Suboccipitals:

A *Rectus Capitis Posterior Major*
Rectus Capitis Posterior Minor
Oblique Capitis Superior
- Rock and tilt the head back into extension

Rectus Capitis Posterior Major
Oblique Capitis Inferior
- Rotate the head to the same side

✤   ✤   ✤

Rectus Capitis Posterior Major

O Spinous process of the axis (C-2)
I Inferior nuchal line of the occiput
N Suboccipital

✤   ✤   ✤

Rectus Capitis Posterior Minor

O Tubercle of the posterior arch of the atlas (C-1)
I Inferior nuchal line of the occiput
N Suboccipital

✤   ✤   ✤

Oblique Capitis Superior

O Transverse process of the atlas (C-1)
I Between the nuchal lines of the occiput
N Suboccipital

✤   ✤   ✤

Oblique Capitis Inferior

O Spinous process of the axis (C-2)
I Transverse process of the atlas (C-1)
N Suboccipital

Rectus capitis posterior major

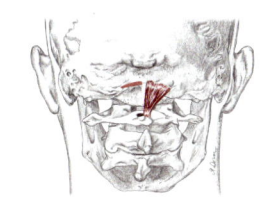

Rectus capitis posterior minor

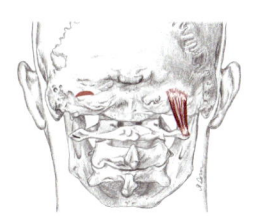

Oblique capitis superior

Oblique capitis inferior

| TGB, 3rd | Backpack | Handbook | DVD |
| p. 211-212 | Spine & Thorax | p. 104-105 | Spine & Thorax |

Suboccipitals

Starter Questions
- What two bony landmarks can help you isolate the suboccipitals? *(superior nuchal line, spinous process of C-2)*
- How can the lateral edge of the upper fibers of the trapezius be helpful in determining the location of the suboccipitals? *(it is the same width)*

ADL
- Appreciating a large painting from a close proximity (small, fine movements of the head and neck)

Two Cents
- Because these muscles are difficult to access, students may get frustrated and "blow them off." Help to keep it in perspective for them: "Yes, they're deep, buried and small, and *still* just below your fingers."
- If students leave this lesson with no palpatory experience other than cradling their partner's head in their hands and sinking their fingers into the suboccipital space - fine. That exercise alone will kinesthetically demonstrate to them (and their soothed, appreciative partners) that muscles don't necessarily need direct contact for a profound effect to occur.

Quadratus Lumborum

A *Unilaterally:*
- Laterally tilt the pelvis
- Laterally flex the vertebral column to the same side
- Assist to extend the vertebral column

Bilaterally:
- Fix the last rib during inhalation and forced exhalation

O Posterior iliac crest

I Last rib, transverse processes of first through fourth lumbar vertebrae

N Branches of first lumbar and twelfth thoracic

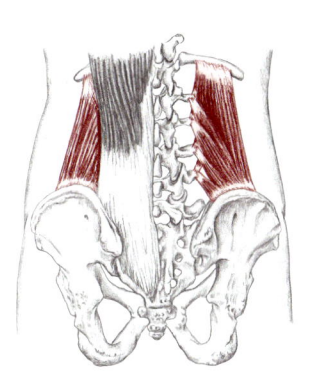

Starter Questions
- What's the nickname of the QL? *("hip hiker")*
- What are two bony landmarks that could help you isolate the quadratus? *(12th rib, TVPs of the lumbar vertebrae, posterior iliac crest)*
- Being deep to the erectors, from which direction could you access the quadratus? *(from the side of the torso)*

ADL
- Elevate the pelvis when walking
- Raising yourself up from a sidelying position (lateral flexion)
- Scratching the outside of your knee (isometric lateral flexion)

Two Cents
- Drawing the QL on the body can be clarifying and informative for students.
- Accessing the QL can be ticklish, so encourage students to explore slowly.
- Sidelying position often offers students a dramatic example of the QL's contractile abilities.
- Students might not be familiar yet with the posterior iliac crest.
- In their enthusiasm, students on the table oftentimes hike their hip with far too much effort; encourage a small, almost imperceptible contraction.

TGB, 3rd p. 213-214	Backpack Spine & Thorax	Handbook p. 106-107	DVD Spine & Thorax

Abdominals

Rectus Abdominis

A Flex the vertebral column
O Pubic crest, pubic symphysis
I Cartilage of fifth, sixth and seventh ribs and xiphoid process
N Branches of intercostals

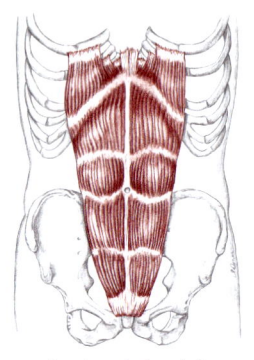

Rectus abdominis

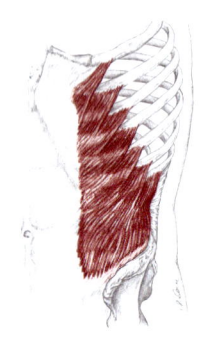

External Oblique

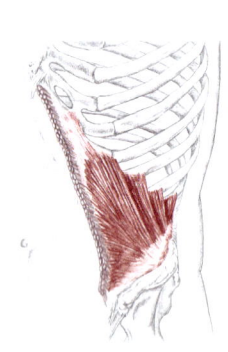

A *Unilaterally:*
- Laterally flex vertebral column to the same side
- Rotate vertebral column to the opposite side

Bilaterally:
- Flex the vertebral column
- Compress abdominal contents

O Lower eight ribs
I Anterior part of the iliac crest, abdominal aponeurosis to linea alba
N Branches of intercostals

External oblique

Internal Oblique

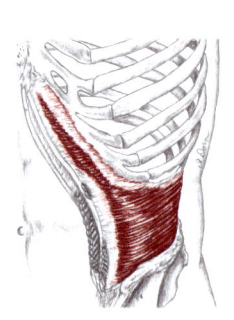

A *Unilaterally:*
- Laterally flex vertebral column to the same side
- Rotate vertebral column to the same side

Bilaterally:
- Flex the vertebral column
- Compress abdominal contents

O Lateral inguinal ligament, iliac crest, thoracolumbar fascia
I Internal surface of lower three ribs, abdominal aponeurosis to linea alba
N Branches of intercostals

Internal oblique

Transverse Abdominis

A Compress abdominal contents
O Lateral inguinal ligament, iliac crest, thoracolumbar fascia and internal surface of lower six ribs
I Abdominal aponeurosis to linea alba
N Branches of intercostals

Transverse abdominis

Abdominals

Starter Questions
- What are names of the four abdominal muscles?
- Which muscle is responsible for that "washboard" contour? *(rectus abdominis)*
- When producing rotation of the trunk, the *right* external oblique is synergistic with which abdominal muscle? *(the **left** internal oblique)*
- The abdominals are antagonists with which group of muscles? *(erector spinae group)*
- Which muscles must you palpate through in order to access the transverse abdominis? *(external and internal obliques)*

ADL
- A sit-up (flexion)
- A Navy Seal sit-up (flexion with rotation)
- When in bed, reaching over for the alarm clock (flexion, rotation)
- Coughing, vomiting, defecation (hopefully not at the same time)

Two Cents
- Students might not be familiar with the pubic crest yet, so before accessing the rectus abdominis, consider a simple demo showing how to access this span of bone.
- Remind students that these muscles cover a surprising amount of surface on the trunk - especially the obliques. Consider recruiting a model to stand as you draw the outline of these broad muscles. Then challenge students to outline the entire mass of these muscles on their partner.

TGB, 3rd p. 215-218	Backpack Spine & Thorax	Handbook p. 106-107	DVD Spine & Thorax

Diaphragm

A
- Draw down the central tendon of diaphragm
- Increase the volume of thoracic cavity during inhalation

O *Costal attachment:*
  Inner surface of lower six ribs
  Lumbar attachment:
  Upper two or three lumbar vertebrae
  Sternal attachment:
  Inner part of xiphoid process

I Central tendon

N Phrenic

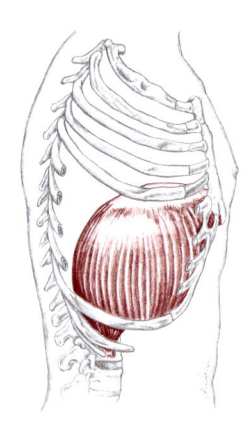

Starter Questions
- The diaphragm divides what two areas of the thorax?
  (upper and lower thoracic cavities)
- Please describe how the diaphragm is involved in respiration.
- Does anyone have any ideas how you could access the diaphragm?

ADL
- Inhaling
- Coughing
- Sneezing
- Hiccuping
- Talking

Two Cents
- The skeleton can be a crucial visual aid to enable students to comprehend the diaphragm's attachments, location and function.
- This is one muscle where a pre-palpation demo that shows proper tempo and finger position can be immensely helpful to students.
- Keep in mind that some students might never have had the underside of their rib cage accessed. Keep an eye out for emotional responses.

TGB, 3rd p. 219-220	Backpack Spine & Thorax	Handbook p. 106-107	DVD Spine & Thorax

78 Instructor's Field Guide

Intercostals

A *External Intercostals:*
- Assist with inhalation by drawing the ribs superiorly, increasing the space of the thoracic cavity

Internal Intercostals:
- Assist with exhalation by drawing the ribs inferiorly, decreasing the space of the thoracic cavity

O Inferior border of the rib above

I Superior border of the rib below

N Intercostal

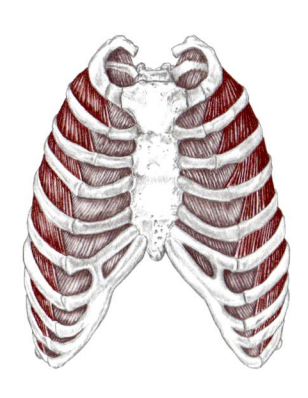

Starter Questions
- Can you name two muscles of the anterior/lateral chest you will need to palpate through to access the intercostals? *(pectoralis major and minor, serratus anterior, latissimus dorsi, external oblique)*
- How are the fibers of the external and internal intercostals arranged in relation to each other? *(perpendicular)*

ADL
- Inhaling
- Coughing
- Sneezing

Two Cents
- Students might need a little encouragement to explore all the way around the ribs (anterior, lateral and posterior surfaces) and work their fingers between the ribs.
- Consider challenging students' perception of these muscles ("they're small and don't do much") by asking them questions: If you collected both groups of intercostals together and laid them out on a table, how large would they be? How would the rib cage function (or not) if we replaced the intercostals with inflexible connective tissue?

TGB, 3rd p. 221	Backpack Spine & Thorax	Handbook p. 106-107	DVD Spine & Thorax

Spine & Thorax

Serratus Posterior Superior & Inferior

Serratus Posterior Superior

A Elevate the ribs during inhalation

O Spinous processes of C-7 to T-3

I Posterior surface of second through fifth ribs

N Spinal nerves one through four

Serratus Posterior Inferior

A Depress the ribs during exhalation

O Spinous processes of T-12 to L-3

I Posterior surface of ninth through twelfth ribs

N Spinal nerves nine through twelve

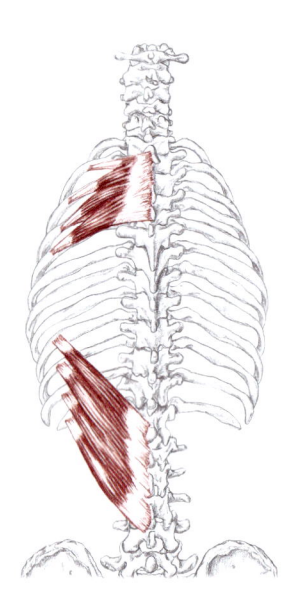

Starter Questions
- Are these muscles deep or superficial to the erector spinae? *(superficial)*
- The serratus posterior superior fibers run parallel to what muscle(s) of the shoulder? *(rhomboids)*
- How is the serratus posterior inferior involved in exhalation? *(depression of the ribs during exhalation)*

ADL
- Inhaling
- Coughing
- Sneezing

Two Cents
- Since these muscles require advanced palpatory skills, consider presenting them at a later date when students are more experienced.
- Drawing the outline of the muscles on one side of the trunk and palpating on the other side can be a helpful visual aid for students.

| TGB, 3rd p. 222 | Backpack Spine & Thorax |

Other Structures

	TGB, 3rd ed.
Ligamentum Nuchae	224
Supraspinous Ligament	225
Abdominal Aorta	225
Thoracolumbar Aponeurosis	226
Craniovertebral Joints	227
Intervertebral Joints	228
Costovertebral Joints	229
Sternocostal Joints	229

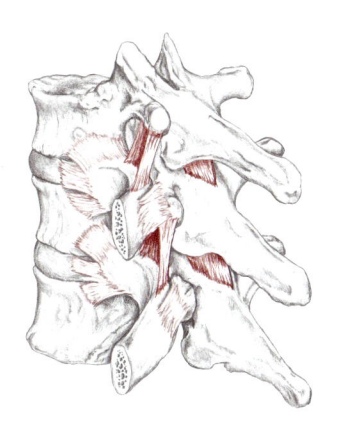

TGB, 3rd p. 224--229	Backpack Spine & Thorax	Handbook p. 108-113

Spine & Thorax 81

5 Head, Neck & Face

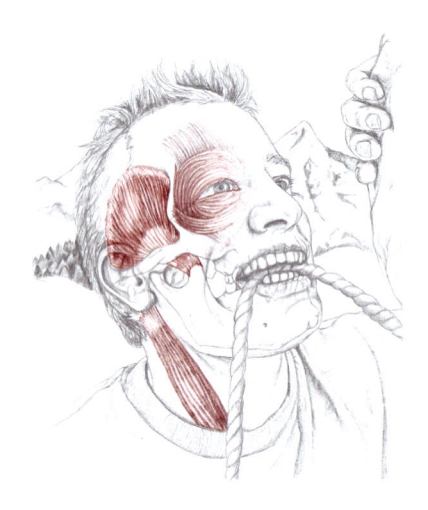

Topography	83
Skin & Fascia	83
Bones	83
Bony Landmark Trails	84
Muscles	85-94
Other Structures	95

Topography

| TGB, 3rd p. 232 | Handbook p. 115 |

Skin & Fascia

| TGB, 3rd p. 233 |

Bones

| TGB, 3rd p. 234-235 | Handbook p. 116-120 |

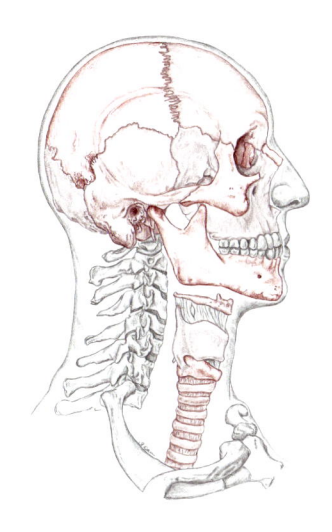

Starter Questions
- How many cranial and facial bones are there?
  (eight cranial, fourteen facial)
- How do the joint structures of the cranial bones differ from the joints of the shoulder and elbow? *(they are fibrous joints woven together with tight-fitting sutures while the shoulder and elbow are synovial [mobile] joints)*

Head, Neck & Face

Bony Landmark Trails

Trail 1 "Around the Globe" palpates the bones and bony landmarks of the cranium and face.

a Occiput
    External occipital protuberance
    Superior nuchal lines
b Parietal
c Temporal
    Mastoid process
    Styloid process
    Zygomatic arch
d Frontal
e Sphenoid
f Nasal, zygomatic and maxilla

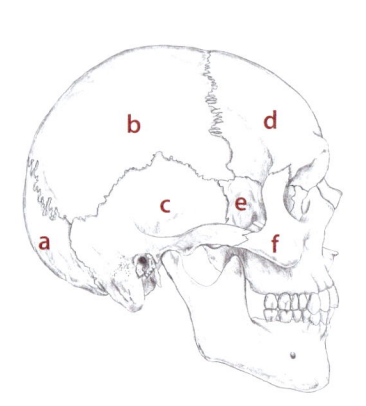

Trail 2 "Jaw Jaunt" explores the mandible.

a Body
b Base
c Submandibular fossa
d Angle
e Ramus
f Coronoid process
g Condyle

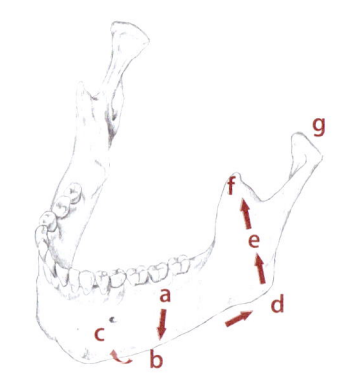

Trail 3 "Horseshoe Trek" locates the cartilaginous structures of the anterior neck and the horseshoe-shaped hyoid bone.

a Trachea
b Cricoid cartilage
c Thyroid cartilage
d Hyoid bone

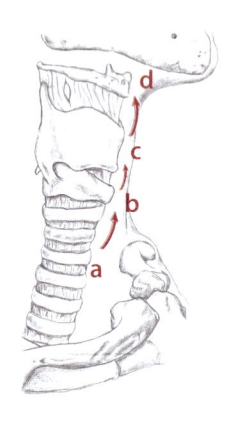

TGB, 3rd
p. 236-245

Muscles of the Head, Neck & Face

Muscle	Field Guide	TGB, 3rd ed.
Infrahyoids	92	261
Masseter	89	256
Occipitofrontalis	93	263
Platysma	94	263
Scalenes	87	252
Sternocleidomastoid	86	250
Suprahyoids & Digastric	91	259
Temporalis	90	257

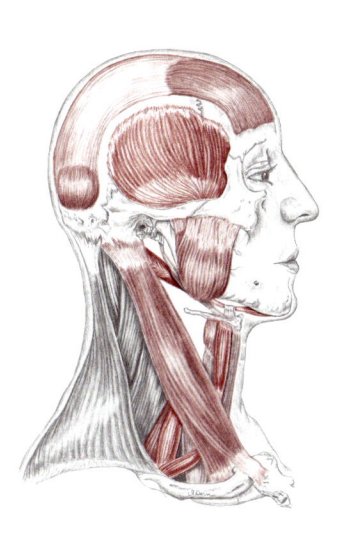

Starter Questions
- What are two powerful muscles involved with mastication (the chewing of food)? *(masseter and temporalis)*
- What are two muscles of the head and neck that are involved with rotation of the cervical spine? *(sternocleidomastoid and scalenes)*

TGB, 3rd p. 246-249	Backpack Head/Neck/Face	Handbook p. 121-131	DVD Head/Neck/Face

Sternocleidomastoid

A *Unilaterally:*
- Laterally flex the head and neck to the same side
- Rotate the head and neck to the opposite side

Bilaterally:
- Flex the neck
- Assist in inhalation (elevation of the rib cage)

O *Sternal head:*
Top of manubrium
Clavicular head:
Medial one-third of the clavicle

I Mastoid process of temporal bone and lateral portion of superior nuchal line of occiput

N Spinal accessory

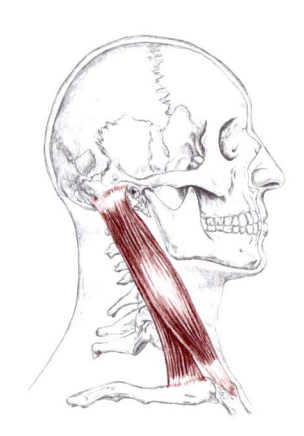

Starter Questions
- Rotating your head to the left would require which of your SCMs? *(the right SCM)*
- What does the name "sternocleidomastoid" tell you about this muscle?
  (where it attaches: sternum [sterno-], clavicle [cleido-] and mastoid process)
- What structure do you need to be aware of when exploring the SCM?
  (the carotid artery)

ADL
- Shake your head "no" (opposite side rotation)
- Shake your head "yes" (bilateral flexion)
- Inhaling while running

Two Cents
- Rotating the head away from the side you're palpating allows the SCM to be grasped with less chance of interfering with the carotid artery.
- Isolating the sternal and clavicular tendons can be challenging for students.

TGB, 3rd p. 250-251	Backpack Head/Neck/Face	Handbook p. 132-133	DVD Head/Neck/Face

Scalenes

Actions of Scalenes

Unilaterally:
- With the ribs fixed, laterally flex the head and neck to the same side (All)
- Rotate head and neck to the opposite side (All)

Bilaterally:
- Elevate the ribs during inhalation (All)
- Flex the head and neck (Anterior)

❈ ❈ ❈

Anterior Scalene

O Transverse processes of third through sixth cervical vertebrae (anterior tubercles)
I First rib
N Cervical and brachial plexuses

❈ ❈ ❈

Middle Scalene

O Transverse processes of second through seventh cervical vertebrae (posterior tubercles)
I First rib
N Cervical and brachial plexuses

❈ ❈ ❈

Posterior Scalene

O Transverse processes of fifth and sixth cervical vertebrae (posterior tubercles)
I Second rib
N Brachial plexus

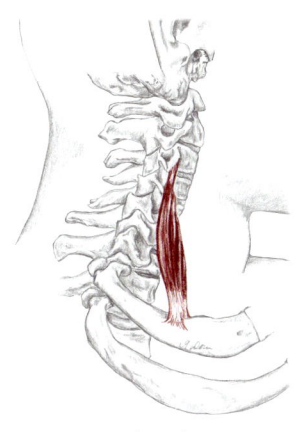

Anterior

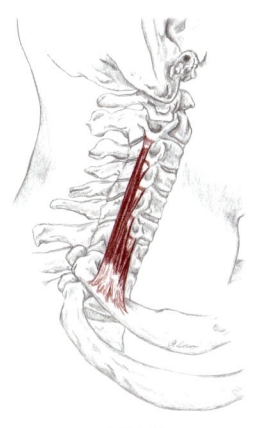

Middle

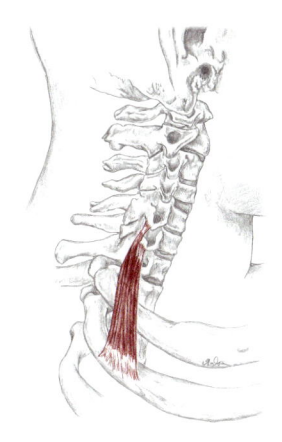

Posterior

Head, Neck & Face

Scalenes

Starter Questions
- As a group, the scalenes are located between which two large, superficial muscles? *(SCM and trapezius)*
- Which structure and vessel pass between the anterior and middle scalenes? *(brachial plexus and subclavian artery)*

ADL
- Taking deep breathes into the upper chest
- Holding a phone with your ear and shoulder (lateral flexion)
- Nod your head "yes" (bilateral flexion by the anterior scalene) and "no" (opposite side rotation by all scalene muscles)

Two Cents
- Consider presenting a brief discussion of thoracic outlet syndrome as you introduce these muscles.
- Since the scalenes can be challenging to visualize on the body, draw the outline of these muscles on a seated model. This is a great way for students to see the scalenes from all perspectives.
- Students might need some reassurance that palpation of the cervical TVPs becomes easier with practice.

TGB, 3rd p. 252-255	Backpack Head/Neck/Face	Handbook p. 132-133	DVD Head/Neck/Face

Masseter

A Elevate the mandible
(temporomandibular joint)

O Zygomatic arch

I Angle and ramus of mandible

N Mandibular nerve via masseteric nerve

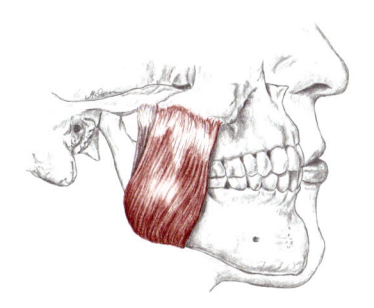

Starter Questions
- What is the masseter's "claim to fame?"
  (It's the strongest muscle in the body relative to size. The bulkiest muscle in the body is the gluteus maximus - about 2.25 lbs; the longest is the sartorius - about 19.5 inches; and the 18-inch external oblique is the widest.)
- What are two bony landmarks that can help isolate the masseter?
  (zygomatic arch, angle/ramus of the mandible)
- The masseter is deep to which gland? *(the parotid)*

ADL
- Chewing food or gum
- Gnashing your teeth during an argument
- Talking

Two Cents
- Sometimes the overlying parotid gland can be tender when exploring the masseter.
- If you have a clean-shaven, bald person in class, take this opportunity to draw the outline of the masseter and temporalis on his head. Then have him chew on a big piece of gum.
- Hand out gum to the whole class!

TGB, 3rd p. 256-257	Backpack Head/Neck/Face	Handbook p. 132-133	DVD Head/Neck/Face

Head, Neck & Face

Temporalis

A
- Elevate the mandible (temporomandibular joint)
- Retract the mandible (temporomandibular joint)

O Temporal fossa and fascia

I Coronoid process of the mandible

N Deep temporal branch of mandibular nerve

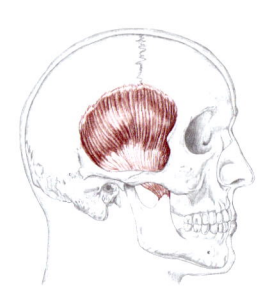

Starter Questions
- What bony landmark of the mandible can help you locate the temporalis' insertion? *(coronoid process)*
- What two actions does the temporalis perform? *(elevate and retract mandible)*
- The temporalis passes beneath what bony arch? *(zygomatic arch)*

ADL
- Biting off a chunk of beef jerky
- Grinding your teeth while you sleep
- Singing

Two Cents
- This seems like a rather straightforward muscle, but students can get confused around the coronoid process.
- Using the skeleton's skull, point out the depth of the space beneath the zygomatic arch. Note for students that the wide space is filled by the temporalis.

TGB, 3rd p. 257-258	Backpack Head/Neck/Face	Handbook p. 132-133	DVD Head/Neck/Face

Suprahyoids & Digastric

Suprahyoids

A
- Elevate hyoid and tongue
- Depress mandible

O *Geniohyoid, Mylohyoid:* Underside of mandible
Stylohyoid: Styloid process

I Hyoid bone

N *Geniohyoid:* Hypoglossal
Mylohyoid: Mylohyoid
Stylohyoid: Facial

Digastric

A
- With hyoid fixed, it depresses the mandible
- With mandible fixed, it elevates the hyoid
- Retracts the mandible (TM joint)

O Mastoid process (deep to sternocleidomastoid and splenius capitis)

I Inferior border of the mandible

N Mylohyoid and facial

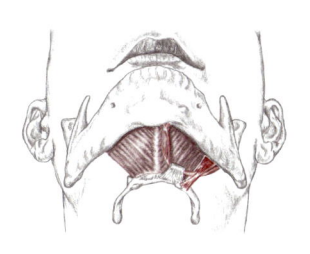

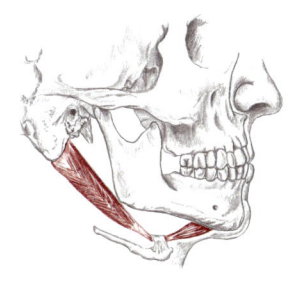

Digastric

Starter Questions
- How many suprahyoids are there and what are their names?
  (four: geniohyoid, mylohyoid, stylohoid, digastric)
- What bony landmarks do you think would be helpful to isolate these muscles?
  (base of mandible, hyoid bone, mastoid process)
- What action could you ask your partner to perform to contract the suprahyoids?
  (depress the mandible)

ADL
- Swallowing
- Gargling
- Speaking

Two Cents
- Students might not yet be familiar with the submandibular gland.
- Keep an eye out for students who inadvertently place their hand(s) in a choke-like position when exploring these muscles. Instruct them to avoid letting their hands cross the centerline of their partner's body; this will prevent such threatening hand maneuvers.

Head, Neck & Face

Infrahyoids

A Depress the hyoid bone and thyroid cartilage

O *Sternohyoid and Sternothyroid:*
   Top of manubrium
   Thyrohyoid: Thyroid cartilage
   Omohyoid: Superior border of the scapula

I *Sternohyoid, Omohyoid and Thyrohyoid:*
   Hyoid bone
   Sternothyroid: Thyroid cartilage

N Upper cervical

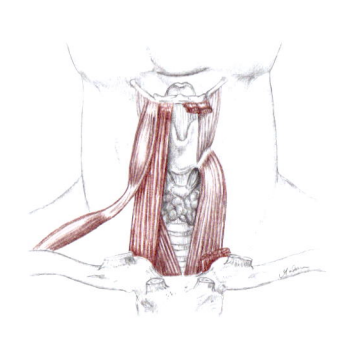

Starter Questions
- How many infrahyoids are there and what are their names?
  (four: sternohyoid, sternothyroid, thyrohyoid, omohyoid)
- What are four structures to be aware of that are directly deep to the infrahyoids? *(thyroid gland, thyroid cartilage, trachea, hyoid bone)*
- Why does the body assign all of these muscles (supra- and infrahyoids) to simply move the hyoid bone? *(have students try to speak or swallow without moving their hyoid bone)*

ADL
- Swallowing
- Speaking (through their opposing action with the suprahyoids)

Two Cents
- The infrahyoids fall in the advanced palpatory category, so you might want to present them at a later date.
- As with the suprahyoids, keep an eye out for students who inadvertently place their hand(s) in a choke-like position when exploring these muscles.

Suprahyoids & Digastric

TGB, 3rd p. 259-260	Backpack Head/Neck/Face	Handbook p. 134-135	DVD Head/Neck/Face

Infrahyoids

TGB, 3rd p. 261-262	Backpack Head/Neck/Face	Handbook p. 134-135	DVD Head/Neck/Face

Occipitofrontalis

A
- *Frontalis:* Raise the eyebrows and wrinkle the forehead
- *Occipitalis:* Anchor and retract the galea posteriorly

O *Both:* Galea aponeurotica

I *Frontalis:* Skin over the eyebrows
Occipitalis: Superior nuchal line of the occiput

N Facial

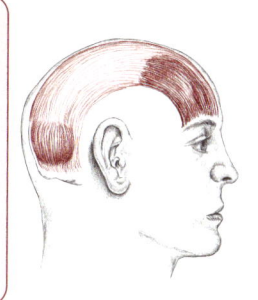

Starter Question
- What is the name of the large sheet of connective tissue that runs between the occipitofrontalis bellies? *(galea aponeurotica)*

ADL
- Raising your eyebrows in shock or surprise
- Wrinkling your forehead while confused
- The occipital belly is also active during smiling and yawning - according to a study of 30 volunteers who allowed electrodes to measure their muscle activity

Two Cents
- A student can feel the galea aponeurotica shift position by setting her fingertips gently on her partner's scalp as her partner raises and lowers his eyebrows.

| TGB, 3rd p. 263-264 | Backpack Head/Neck/Face | Handbook p. 134-135 |

Platysma

A • Assist in depression of the mandible (temporomandibular joint)
  • Tighten the fascia of the neck

O Fascia covering superior part of pectoralis major

I Base of mandible, skin of lower part of face

N Facial

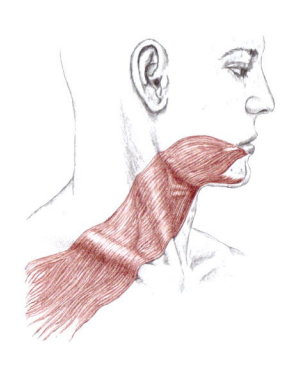

Starter Question
• Who can do a "Creature from the Black Lagoon" expression?

ADL
• Frowning or pouting (drawing the corners of the mouth down)
• Saying "Ahh" at the dentist (assist in depressing the mandible)
• General, abject expression of terror

| TGB, 3rd p. 263 | Backpack Head/Neck/Face | Handbook p. 134-135 |

Pterygoids - Medial & Lateral

| TGB, 3rd p. 265 | Backpack Head/Neck/Face | Handbook p. 134-135 |

Longus Capitis and Colli

| TGB, 3rd p. 266 | Backpack Head/Neck/Face | Handbook p. 134-135 |

Other Structures

	TGB, 3rd ed.
Common Carotid Artery	268
Temporal Artery	268
Facial Artery	268
Facial Nerve	269
Vertebral Artery	269
Parotid Gland and Duct	269
Submandibular Gland	269
Thyroid Gland	270
Cervical Lymph Nodes	271
Brachial Plexus	271

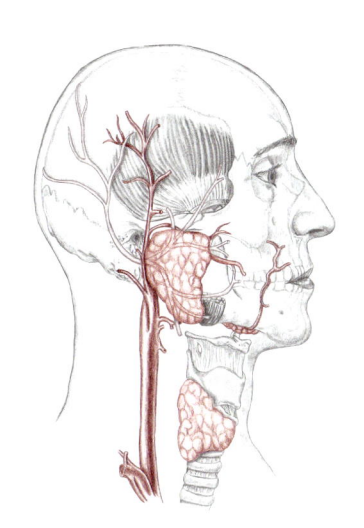

TGB, 3rd p. 267-271	Backpack Head/Neck/Face	Handbook p. 136

6 Pelvis & Thigh

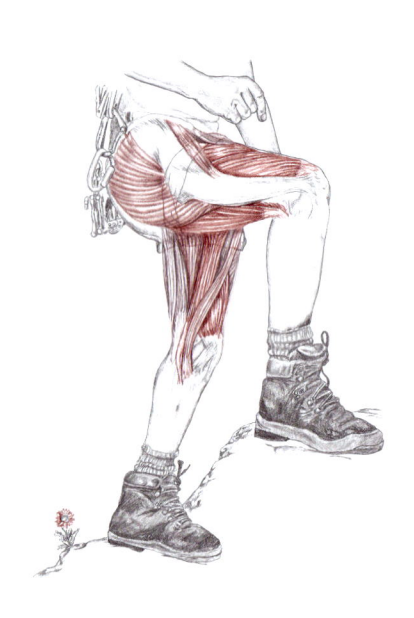

Topography	97
Skin & Fascia	97
Bones	97
Bony Landmark Trails	98-99
Muscles	100-112
Other Structures	113

Topography

| TGB, 3rd p. 274 | Handbook p. 137 |

Skin & Fascia

| TGB, 3rd p. 275 |

Bones

| TGB, 3rd p. 276-281 | Handbook p. 138-143 |

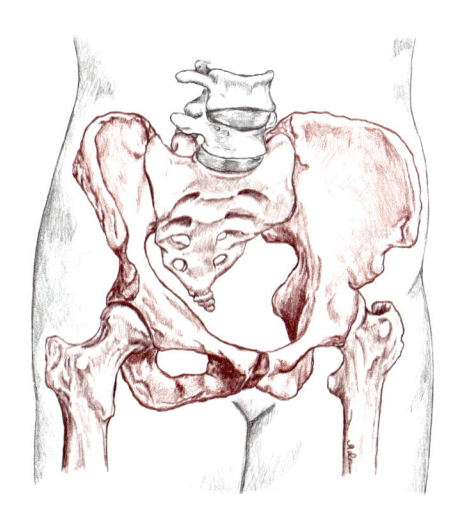

Starter Questions
- The pelvis consists of which two bones? *(two hip bones)*
- What are the three bones that fuse together to form a hip? *(ilium, ischium, pubis)*
- What type of joint is the coxal joint? *(ball-and-socket)*

Two Cents
- For understandable reasons, palpating (and being palpated) in the areas of the groin, coccyx and ischial tuberosity might create some anxiety among students. Consider a slow, thorough pre-palpation demonstration before students access these areas.

Pelvis & Thigh

Bony Landmark Trails

Trail 1 "Solo Pass" - students palpate the prominent landmarks of their own pelvis.

a Anterior superior iliac spine (ASIS)
b Iliac crest
c Posterior superior iliac spine (PSIS)
d Pubic crest
e Ischial tuberosity
f Greater trochanter

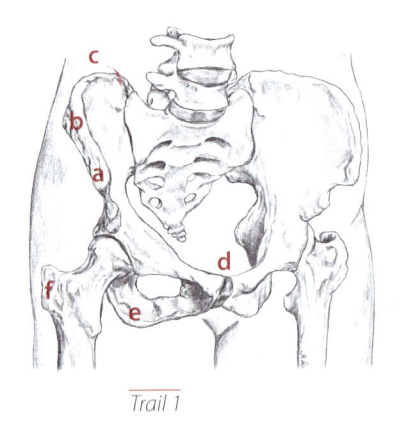

Trail 1

Trail 2 "Iliac Avenue" travels along the superior aspect of the pelvis on the ilium.

a Anterior superior iliac spine (ASIS)
b Anterior inferior iliac spine (AIIS)
c Iliac crest
d Iliac fossa
e Posterior superior iliac spine (PSIS)

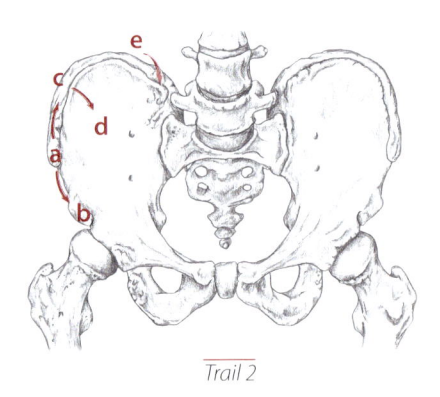

Trail 2

TGB, 3rd
p. 282-293

Bony Landmark Trails

Trail 3 "Tailbone Trail" accesses the bones at the base of the spine.

a Posterior superior iliac spine (PSIS)
b Sacrum
c Medial sacral crest
d Edge of the sacrum
e Coccyx
f Sacroiliac joint

Trail 4 "Hip Hike" explores the lateral hip and landmarks of the proximal femur.

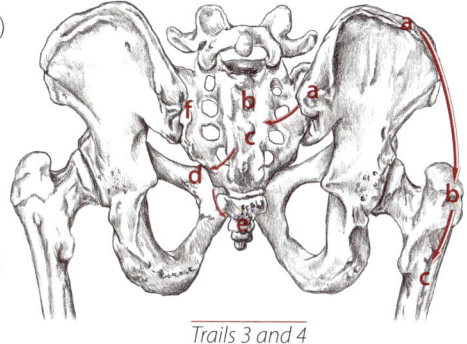

a Iliac crest
b Greater trochanter
c Gluteal tuberosity

Trails 3 and 4

Trail 5 "The Underpass" follows around the pubic region to access the landmarks of the medial thigh.

a Umbilicus
b Pubic crest and tubercles
c Superior ramus of the pubis
d Inferior ramus of pubis and ramus of ischium
e Ischial tuberosity

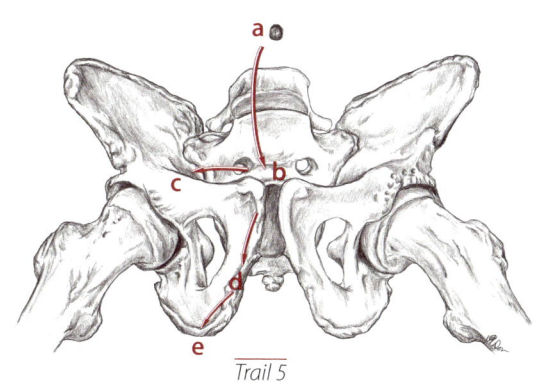

Trail 5

Pelvis & Thigh

Muscles of the Pelvis & Thigh

	Field Guide	TGB, 3rd ed.
Adductor Group	106	313
Gluteals	104	309
Hamstrings	102	305
Iliopsoas	112	326
Lateral Rotators of the Hip	110	322
Quadriceps Femoris Group	101	300
Sartorius	109	320
Tensor Fasciae Latae	108	318

Starter Questions

- The majority of the muscles of the pelvis and thigh can be divided into five groups. What are they? *(quadriceps, hamstrings, gluteals, adductors and lateral rotators)*
- The muscles of the pelvis and thigh create movement at primarily which two joints? *(coxal and tibiofemoral)*
- Which muscle group is an antagonist group to the hamstrings? *(quadriceps - extension of the knee)*
- Which group are antagonists to the gluteals? *(adductors - adduction of the hip)*

TGB, 3rd p. 294-299	Backpack Pelvis & Thigh	Handbook p. 144-157	DVD Pelvis & Thigh

Quadriceps Femoris Group

A *All:*
- Extend the knee (tibiofemoral joint)

Rectus Femoris:
- Flex the hip (coxal joint)

O *Rectus Femoris:*
Anterior inferior iliac spine (AIIS)

Vastus Lateralis:
Lateral lip of linea aspera, gluteal tuberosity

Vastus Medialis:
Medial lip of linea aspera

Vastus Intermedius:
Anterior and lateral shaft of the femur

I Tibial tuberosity

N Femoral

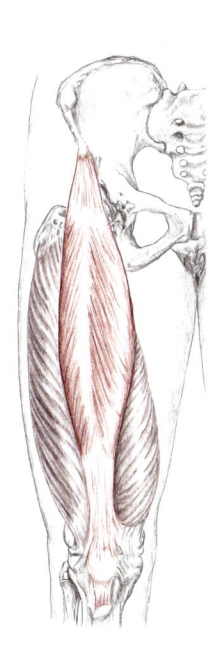

Starter Questions
- What are the names of the four quadriceps? *(rectus femoris, vastus medialis, vastus lateralis, vastus intermedius)*
- What two bony landmarks would help you isolate the rectus femoris? *(AIIS, patella or tibial tuberosity)*
- Why do you think the body would assign four large muscles to primarily perform one action - extension of the knee?

ADL
- Climbing up a flight of stairs
- Stabilizing yourself in a stationary squat position
- Raising your knee quickly into a bad guy's cojones (rectus femoris)

Two Cents
- Students often perceive the quads as only residing on the anterior thigh. You might need to reinforce the fact that they are actually on the anterior, medial and lateral surfaces.
- Students might believe the quads begin at the hemline of a person's shorts. Not so. With a model supine and well draped, dispel this notion by using a washable marker to trace the entire span of the quads. Students will have a new appreciation of the length of these muscles.

TGB, 3rd p. 300-304	Backpack Pelvis & Thigh	Handbook p. 158-159	DVD Pelvis & Thigh

Pelvis & Thigh

Hamstrings

Biceps Femoris

A
- Flex the knee (tibiofemoral joint)
- Laterally rotate the flexed knee (t/f joint)
- Extend the hip (coxal joint)
- Laterally rotate the hip (coxal joint)
- Tilt the pelvis posteriorly

O *Long head of Biceps Femoris:*
   Ischial tuberosity
Short head of Biceps Femoris:
   Lateral lip of linea aspera

I Head of the fibula

N Tibial and peroneal

Biceps (long head)    Biceps (short head)

Semitendinosus

A
- Flex the knee (tibiofemoral joint)
- Medially rotate the flexed knee (t/f joint)
- Extend the hip (coxal joint)
- Medially rotate the hip (coxal joint)
- Tilt the pelvis posteriorly

O Ischial tuberosity

I Proximal, medial shaft of the tibia at pes anserinus tendon

N Tibial

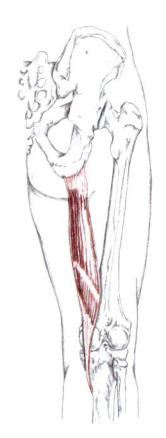

Semitendinosus

Semimembranosus

A
- Flex the knee (tibiofemoral joint)
- Medially rotate the flexed knee (t/f joint)
- Extend the hip (coxal joint)
- Medially rotate the hip (coxal joint)
- Tilt the pelvis posteriorly

O Ischial tuberosity

I Posterior aspect of medial condyle of tibia

N Tibial

Semimembranosus

Hamstrings

Starter Questions
- What are the names of the three hamstrings?
- How can you recall that the semi**T**endinosus is superficial to the semimembranosus? *(it's on **T**op)*
- What bony landmark helps locate the origin of the hamstrings? *(ischial tuberosity)*

ADL
- Running, cycling, swimming, climbing stairs
- Tying your shoes (an isometric contraction)
- Scraping mud off your boots (extension of the hip)

Two Cents
- The hamstrings are an easy group on which to lay one's hands. Students become more challenged when isolating the individual bellies.
- The depression felt between the edges of the biceps femoris and the vastus lateralis can serve as an opportunity for students to feel how far the lateralis extends posteriorly.
- Students might not yet be familiar with the head of the fibula.

TGB, 3rd	Backpack	Handbook	DVD
p. 305-308	Pelvis & Thigh	p. 158-159	Pelvis & Thigh

Pelvis & Thigh

Gluteals

Gluteus Maximus

A *All fibers:*
- Extend the hip (coxal joint)
- Laterally rotate the hip (coxal joint)
- Abduct the hip (coxal joint)

Lower fibers:
- Adduct the hip (coxal joint)

O Coccyx, edge of sacrum, posterior iliac crest, sacrotuberous and sacroiliac ligaments

I Gluteal tuberosity (upper fibers) and iliotibial tract (lower fibers)

N Inferior gluteal

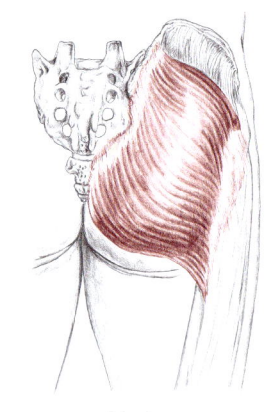

Maximus

Gluteus Medius

A *All fibers:*
- Abduct the hip (coxal joint)

Anterior fibers:
- Flex the hip (coxal joint)
- Medially rotate the hip (coxal joint)

Posterior fibers:
- Extend the hip (coxal joint)
- Laterally rotate the hip (coxal joint)

O Gluteal surface of the ilium between the iliac crest and the posterior and anterior gluteal lines

I Greater trochanter

N Superior gluteal

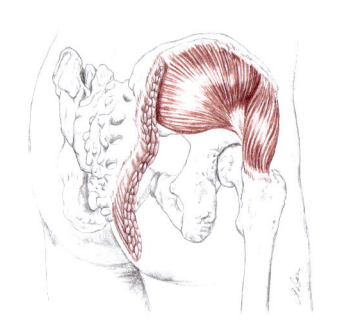

Medius

TGB, 3rd p. 309-312	Backpack Pelvis & Thigh	Handbook p. 160-161	DVD Pelvis & Thigh

Instructor's Field Guide

Gluteus Minimus

A
- Abduct the hip (coxal joint)
- Medially rotate the hip (coxal joint)
- Flex the hip (coxal joint)

O Gluteal surface of the ilium between the anterior and inferior gluteal lines

I Anterior border of greater trochanter

N Superior gluteal

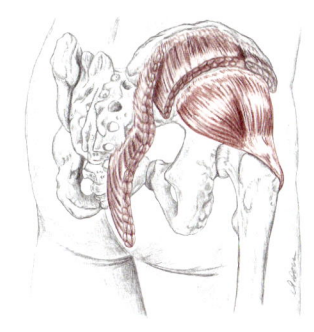

Minimus

Starter Questions
- What three bony landmarks could help you isolate the borders of the gluteus maximus? *(coccyx, posterior sacrum and PSIS)*
- The maximus and medius are synergists with the hamstrings during what action? *(extension of the hip)*
- Why do you think the gluteus medius is able to rotate the hip both medially and laterally? *(has a broad origin; has convergent fibers; the ball-and-socket coxal joint offers a wide range of motion)*

ADL
- Climbing stairs (maximus, especially)
- Running, cycling, swimming, skating
- Latin dancing (lots of lateral rotation of the hip)

Two Cents
- Keep in mind that students might feel uncomfortable exploring this area on a classmate. Keep an eye out for giggling and other emotional outbursts.
- Students assume these are "posterior" muscles, but encourage them to try a sidelying position for full access of the medius and minimus.

Adductor Group

A *All:*
- Adduct the hip (coxal joint)
- Medially rotate the hip (coxal joint)

All, except Gracilis:
- Assist to flex the hip (coxal joint)

Gracilis:
- Flex the knee (tibiofemoral joint)
- Medially rotate the flexed knee (t/f joint)

Posterior fibers of Adductor Magnus:
- Extend the hip (coxal joint)

Adductor Magnus

O Inferior ramus of the pubis, ramus of ischium and ischial tuberosity
I Medial lip of linea aspera and adductor tubercle
N Obturator and tibial

Adductor Longus

O Pubic tubercle
I Medial lip of linea aspera
N Obturator

Adductor Brevis

O Inferior ramus of pubis
I Pectineal line and medial lip of linea aspera
N Obturator

Pectineus

O Superior ramus of pubis
I Pectineal line of femur
N Femoral and obturator

Gracilis

O Inferior ramus of pubis and ramus of ischium
I Proximal, medial shaft of tibia at pes anserinus tendon
N Obturator

Group

Magnus

Longus

Brevis

Pectineus

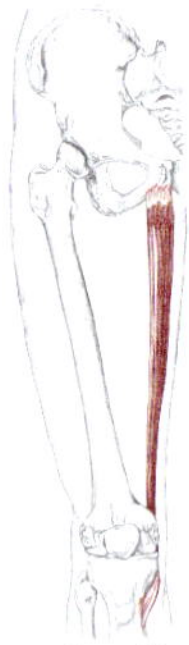

Gracilis

Adductor Group

Starter Questions
- How many adductors are there and what are their names?
- Who has ever suffered from a "groin pull?"
- What bony landmarks of the pelvis will help to access the origins of the adductors? *(superior and inferior rami of the pubis, pubic tubercle, ischial tuberosity)*

ADL
- Ice-skating (doing a cross-over step when turning)
- Gripping a horse with your thighs when riding
- Stabilizing the pelvis when walking

Two Cents
- Like the gluteals, the adductors can present an uncomfortable challenge for students - especially the proximal tendons.
- Create a safe and confident environment by performing a demonstration before students palpate. Begin by accessing the muscles as a group, then the specific bellies and finally the tendinous origins. A slow pace, calm demeanor and steady hands can get students started in the right direction.

TGB, 3rd p. 313-317	Backpack Pelvis & Thigh	Handbook p. 160-161	DVD Pelvis & Thigh

Tensor Fasciae Latae

A
- Flex the hip (coxal joint)
- Medially rotate the hip (coxal joint)
- Abduct the hip (coxal joint)

O Iliac crest, posterior to the ASIS

I Iliotibial tract

N Superior gluteal

Starter Questions
- Looking at its name, what information can you gather about this muscle? *(it tenses the lateral fascia)*
- How are the iliotibial tract fibers different from the vastus lateralis fibers? *(they're superficial and run vertically, where the lateralis fibers run at an oblique angle)*
- What are the three actions of the TFL and what muscle is an exact synergist with it? *(flex, medially rotate and abduct the hip; gluteus minimus)*

ADL
- Running, bicycling, squatting
- Raising your leg to climb into a car (you must flex, medially rotate and abduct the hip)
- The windup for a karate side kick (again, all three movements)

Two Cents
- Palpation of the TFL can be done supine, but sidelying is really the best position.
- For the sake of clarity, anatomy texts (*Trail Guide* included) present the iliotibial tract as having clearly defined edges. This is not accurate. Have students explore the thigh's lateral fascia and experience how it thickens to become the IT tract. This is a fine exercise to enable them to sense the omnipresence of fascia.

TGB, 3rd p. 318-319	Backpack Pelvis & Thigh	Handbook p. 162-164	DVD Pelvis & Thigh

Instructor's Field Guide

Sartorius

A
- Flex the hip (coxal joint)
- Laterally rotate the hip (coxal joint)
- Abduct the hip (coxal joint)

- Flex the knee (tibiofemoral joint)
- Medially rotate the flexed knee (tibiofemoral joint)

O Anterior superior iliac spine (ASIS)

I Proximal, medial shaft of the tibia (pes anserinus tendon)

N Femoral

Starter Questions
- The sartorius extends the length of what bone without making contact? *(femur)*
- Which muscles insert at the pes anserinus attachment site? *(sartorius, gracilis and semitendinosus)*
- What bony landmark of the pelvis can help locate the top portion of the sartorius? *(ASIS)*

ADL
- Folding yourself into a lotus position for meditation
- Sitting in a tailor position (common among men)
- Crossing and uncrossing your legs (common among both sexes)

Two Cents
- The sartorius can be like a snake - it seems to slip from your fingers.
- Bringing a measuring tape to class can be a fun exercise to measure the longest muscle in the body. What's the difference between its shortened and lengthened positions?
- Students can become confused by the pes anserinus tendon – is it one tendon or three? Clarify for them how these three tendons merge as one.

TGB, 3rd p. 320	Backpack Pelvis & Thigh	Handbook p. 162-164	DVD Pelvis & Thigh

Pelvis & Thigh

Lateral Rotators of the Hip

Piriformis

A
- Laterally rotate the hip (coxal joint)
- Abduct the hip when the hip is flexed

O Anterior surface of sacrum

I Greater trochanter

N Branch of sacral plexus

Quadratus Femoris

A Laterally rotate the hip (coxal joint)

O Lateral border of ischial tuberosity

I Intertrochanteric crest, between the greater and lesser trochanters

N Branch of sacral plexus

Obturator Internus

A Laterally rotate the hip (coxal joint)

O Obturator membrane and inferior surface of obturator foramen

I Medial surface of greater trochanter

N Branch of sacral plexus

Obturator Externus

A Laterally rotate the hip (coxal joint)

O Superior and inferior rami of pubis

I Trochanteric fossa of femur

N Obturator

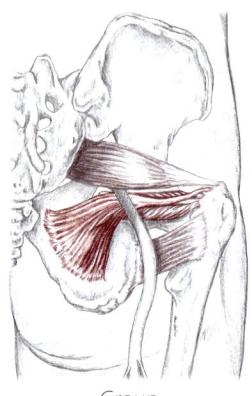

Group

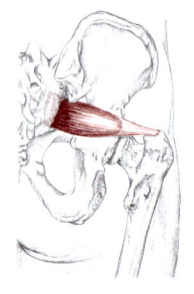

Piriformis

Quadratus femoris

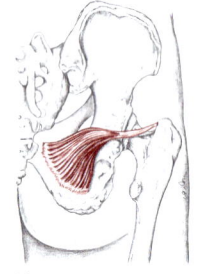

Obturator internus

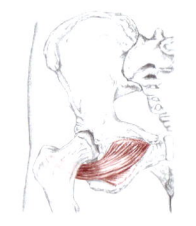

Obturator externus

Lateral Rotators of the Hip

Gemellus Superior
A Laterally rotate the hip (coxal joint)
O Ischial spine
I Upper border of greater trochanter
N Branch of sacral plexus

❋ ❋ ❋

Gemellus Inferior
A Laterally rotate the hip (coxal joint)
O Ischial tuberosity
I Upper border of greater trochanter
N Branch of sacral plexus

Gemellus superior

Gemellus inferior

Starter Questions
- How many lateral rotators are there and what are their names?
  (six; piriformis, quadratus femoris, obturator internus, obturator externus, gemellus superior, gemellus inferior)
- What large vessel do you need to consider when accessing the piriformis?
  (sciatic nerve)
- What three bony landmarks can help you isolate the piriformis?
  (coccyx, PSIS and greater trochanter)

ADL
- Holding the pelvis stable while standing (primarily by the piriformis)
- Walking, running, hiking, swimming, climbing, dodgeball
- Shuffling in front of a row of seated patrons while getting to your concert seat

Two Cents
- *Trail Guide* focuses only on the piriformis and the quadratus femoris since they're the most accessible of the rotators. The gemelli and obturators are best saved as a later palpatory experience.
- Consider a well-paced and confidence-building demo before students palpate.
- Drawing the outline of the piriformis and quadratus femoris on a model can help students visualize these muscles.

TGB, 3rd p. 322-325	Backpack Pelvis & Thigh	Handbook p. 162-164	DVD Pelvis & Thigh

Iliopsoas

Psoas Major

A
- Flex the hip (coxal joint)
- Laterally rotate the hip (coxal joint)
- Adduct the hip (coxal joint)

O Bodies and transverse processes of lumbar vertebrae

I Lesser trochanter

N Lumbar plexus

Psoas major

Iliacus

A
- Flex the hip (coxal joint)
- Laterally rotate the hip (coxal joint)
- Adduct the hip (coxal joint)

O Iliac fossa

I Lesser trochanter

N Femoral

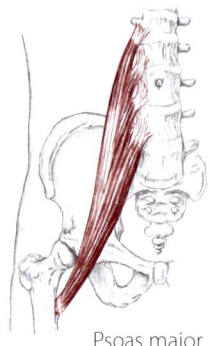

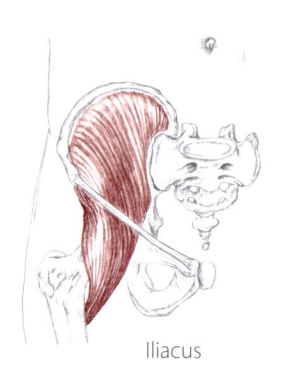

Iliacus

Starter Questions
- What bony ridge could you start at to locate the iliacus? *(iliac crest)*
- What muscles will you palpate through to reach the psoas and iliacus? *(external oblique, internal oblique and transverse abdominis)*

ADL
- Hiking, climbing or walking up an incline
- Getting up from a reclined position (the movement of a small sit-up)
- Reaching up, against gravity, to untie the ropes around your ankles that suspend you upside down from a tree limb *(it could happen)*

Two Cents
- Like the adductors and gluteals, a pre-table demonstration can answer many questions and prepare students for palpation.
- Keep in mind that most students might never have had their abdomen explored in this way. Look for comfortable positioning on the table and slow, gentle hand movements.
- Consider mentioning that accessing the iliopsoas can create an urge in their partner to "release gas." Get this out in the open, before you-know-what does.

TGB, 3rd p. 326-329	Backpack Pelvis & Thigh	Handbook p. 162-164	DVD Pelvis & Thigh

Instructor's Field Guide

Other Structures

	TGB, 3rd ed.
Femoral Triangle	330
Ligaments of Pelvis	331
Ligaments of Coxal Joint	332
Inguinal Ligament	333
Femoral Artery, Nerve and Vein	333
Inguinal Lymph Nodes	334
Sacrotuberous Ligament	334
Posterior Sacroiliac Ligaments	334
Iliolumbar Ligament	335
Sciatic Nerve	335

TGB, 3rd	Backpack	Handbook
p. 330-336	Pelvis & Thigh	p. 165-169

7 Leg & Foot

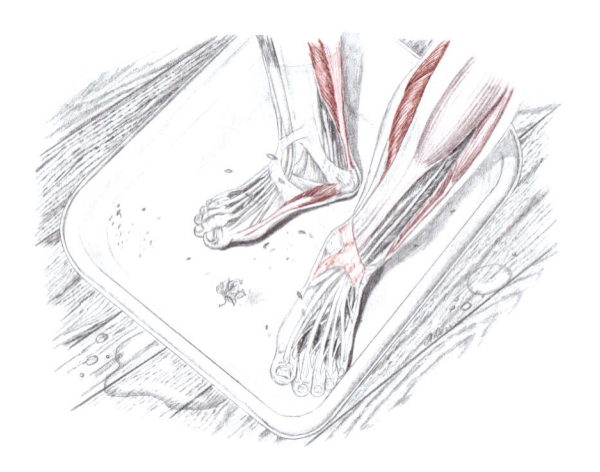

Topography	115
Skin & Fascia	115
Bones	115
Bony Landmark Trails	116-117
Muscles	118-129
Other Structures	130

Topography

| TGB, 3rd p. 338 | Handbook p. 171 |

Skin & Fascia

| TGB, 3rd p. 339 |

Bones of the Knee & Leg

| TGB, 3rd p. 340-342 | Handbook p. 172-174 |

Bones of the Ankle and Foot

| TGB, 3rd p. 348-349 | Handbook p. 175-178 |

Starter Questions

- How many tarsals are there and can you name them?
  (five: medial, middle and lateral cuneiforms, navicular and cuboid)
- What is the proper name of the "ankle" joint? *(talocrural)*
- Which bone of the leg supports virtually all of the weight of the body and is palpable from top to bottom? *(tibia)*

Leg & Foot

Bony Landmark Trails of the Knee

Trail 1 "Landmark Trail" links together the most prominent landmarks of the knee.

a   Patella
b   Tibial tuberosity
c   Shaft of the tibia
d   Head of the fibula

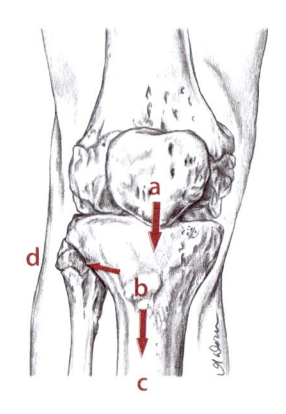

Trail 2 "Waddle Walk" has two paths exploring the medial and lateral aspects of the proximal tibia. It ends at the pes anserinus ("goose foot" in Latin) attachment site.

a   Patella
b   Medial and lateral tibial plateaus
c   Pes anserinus attachment site

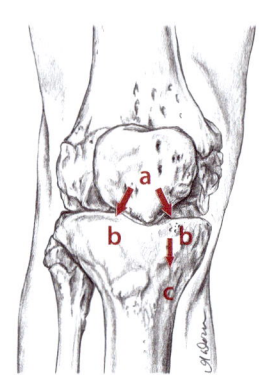

Trail 3 "Hills on Both Sides" explores the bumps of the distal end of the femur.

a   Edge of the medial and lateral femoral condyles
b   Medial and lateral epicondyles of the femur
c   Adductor tubercle

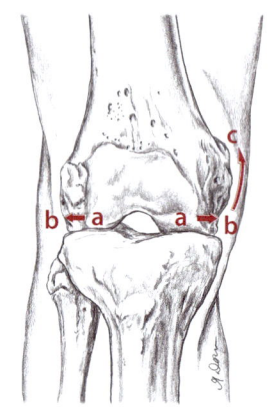

Patella removed

TGB, 3rd
p. 343-347

116 Instructor's Field Guide

Bony Landmark Trails of the Ankle and Foot

Trail 1 "The Back Road" locates the bones and landmarks of the hind foot and ankle.

a Lateral and medial malleoli
b Malleolar grooves
c Calcaneus
   Tuberosity of calcaneus
   Sustentaculum tali
   Peroneal tubercle
d Talus
   Head
   Trochlea
   Medial tubercle

Trail 2 This route, "Little Piggies," palpates the bones and joints of the toes and forefoot.

a Hallucis
b First metatarsal
c Second through fifth phalanges
d Second through fifth metatarsals
e Tuberosity of fifth metatarsal

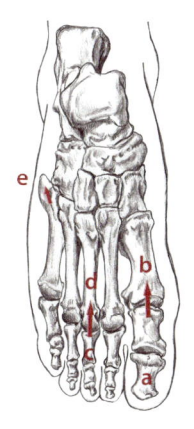

Trail 3 "The Archway" explores the bones of the midfoot located at the arch of the foot.

a Navicular and navicular tuberosity
b Medial, middle and lateral cuneiforms
c Cuboid

TGB, 3rd
p. 350-359

Leg & Foot

Muscles of the Leg & Foot

	Field Guide	**TGB, 3rd ed.**
Extensors of the Ankle and Toes	124	371
Flexors of the Ankle and Toes	126	374
Gastrocnemius	119	364
Muscles of the Foot	128	377
Peroneus Longus and Brevis	123	369
Plantaris	121	367
Popliteus	122	368
Soleus	120	364

Starter Questions
- The majority of the muscles of the leg can be divided into which four groups?
  (gastrocnemius/soleus, peroneals, extensors and flexors of the leg and foot)
- What are the two large muscles that comprise the "calf?"
  (gastrocnemius and soleus)
- What thick span of connective tissue is found along the posterior ankle?
  (calcaneal tendon)

TGB, 3rd p. 360-363	Backpack Leg & Foot	Handbook p. 179-187	DVD Leg & Foot

Instructor's Field Guide

Gastrocnemius

A
- Flex the knee (tibiofemoral joint)
- Plantar flex the ankle (talocrural joint)

O Condyles of the femur, posterior surfaces

I Calcaneus via calcaneal tendon

N Tibial

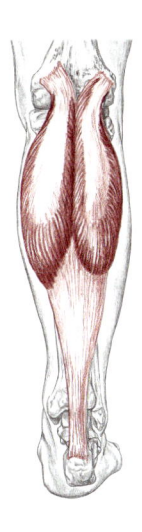

Starter Questions
- The gastrocnemius heads emerge from the posterior knee between which tendons? *(the hamstrings)*
- With your partner standing, what common action could you ask her to perform to contract the gastrocnemius? *("stand on your toes")*
- How does the size of the gastrocnemius compare to the soleus - larger, smaller, the same? *(smaller and quite thin comparatively)*

ADL
- Walking, running, climbing, cycling, swimming
- Peeking over a fence (standing on your toes)
- Riding "English style" on a horse (plantar flexing the ankle, stabilizing the flexed knee)

Two Cents
- Consider asking a student to model these muscles for the class. Then ask another student to draw the gastrocnemius bellies on the model's leg.
- Flexing the knee (in a prone position) can give students an opportunity to feel how the gastrocnemius is disengaged when their partner plantar flexes their ankle.

TGB, 3rd p. 364-366	Backpack Leg & Foot	Handbook p. 188-189	DVD Leg & Foot

Leg & Foot

Soleus

A Plantar flex the ankle (talocrural joint)

O Soleal line, posterior surface of tibia and proximal, posterior surface of fibula

I Calcaneus via calcaneal tendon

N Tibial

Starter Questions
- What muscles comprise the "triceps surae?" *(gastrocnemius and soleus)*
- How can you directly access the soleus if it's deep to the gastrocnemius? *(its medial and lateral edges bulge out the sides of the leg)*
- Why do you think the body would assign this strong muscle a single action that involves a relatively small range of motion? *(how much locomotor movement could you accomplish without strong, repetitive plantar flexion?)*

ADL
- Walking, running, climbing, cycling, swimming
- Setting a heavy lawn mower into the back of a tall pickup truck (plantar flexion with strength and balance)
- Hiking with a backpack (again, plantar flexion with strength and balance)

Two Cents
- Students don't always notice how the soleus bulges out the sides of the leg and is palpable from the leg's anterior surface.
- Remind students that the density of the calf is primarily from the soleus, not the gastrocnemius.
- Take advantage of the calcaneal tendon's easy access – a great opportunity for students to compare different types of tissue and to feel how the tendon becomes steel-like when it's under strain.

TGB, 3rd p. 364-366	Backpack Leg & Foot	Handbook p. 188-189	DVD Leg & Foot

Plantaris

A
- Weak plantar flexion of the ankle (talocrural joint)
- Weak flexion of the knee (tibiofemoral joint)

O Lateral condyle of femur

I Calcaneus via calcaneal tendon

N Tibial

Starter Questions
- For what reason would the plantaris be in the *Guinness Book of World Records*? *(longest tendon in the body)*
- The plantaris can be located between the heads of which muscle? *(gastrocnemius)*
- What bony landmark would you first want to locate to palpate the plantaris? *(head of the fibula, moving medially into the popliteal space)*

Two Cents
- Sometimes the plantaris can be challenging to access, so you might consider presenting it at a later date.

TGB, 3rd p. 367	Backpack Leg & Foot	Handbook p. 188-189

Leg & Foot

Popliteus

A
- Medially rotate the flexed knee (tibiofemoral joint)
- Flex the knee (tibiofemoral joint)

O Lateral epicondyle of the femur

I Proximal, posterior aspect of tibia

N Tibial

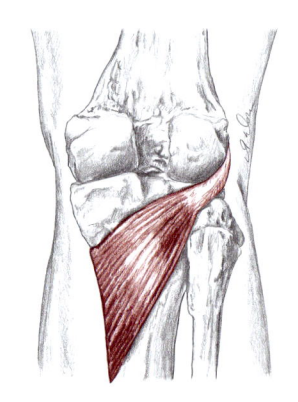

Starter Questions
- What is the nickname of the popliteus? *("the key that unlocks the knee")*
- The popliteus lies deep to which two muscles? *(gastrocnemius and plantaris)*
- Since it is such a deep muscle, how would you access the popliteus? *(from the medial side of the leg, palpating under the soleus)*

ADL
- "Unlocking" the knee from an extended position
- While sitting, crossing one leg over the other and holding your leg and foot in an aristocratic position (medial rotation of the flexed knee)

Two Cents
- Since it is virtually buried and inaccessible, the popliteus is certainly an advanced palpatory experience. You might consider teaching it after students feel more confident in their skills.

TGB, 3rd p. 368	Backpack Leg & Foot	Handbook p. 188-189	DVD Leg & Foot

122 Instructor's Field Guide

Peroneus Longus and Brevis

Peroneus Longus

A
- Evert the foot
- Assist to plantar flex the ankle (talocrural joint)

O Proximal two-thirds of lateral fibula

I Base of the first metatarsal and medial cuneiform

N Superior peroneal

Peroneus Brevis

A
- Evert the foot
- Assist to plantar flex the ankle (talocrural joint)

O Distal two-thirds of lateral fibula

I Tuberosity of fifth metatarsal

N Superior peroneal

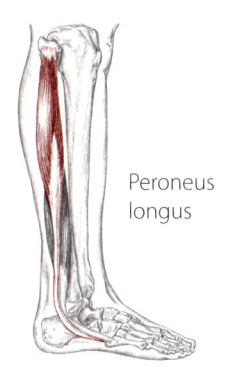

Peroneus longus

Peroneus brevis

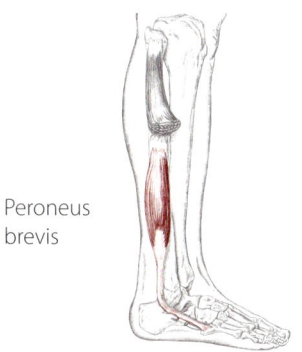

Starter Questions
- The peroneals perform what crucial movement of the foot? *(eversion)*
- What two bony landmarks could help you isolate these muscles? *(head of the fibula, lateral malleolus)*

ADL
- Scraping mud off the inside edge of your boot (eversion of the ankle)
- Hiking on a rocky trail (small, specific stabilizing movements of the foot)
- Skating or skate skiing (eversion occurring at the end of a stroke)

Two Cents
- The peroneals "present" very well on most legs and can be fun to access.
- Try pointing out to students the "dimple" that can often be seen halfway down the lateral sides of the leg when the peroneals contract during eversion.
- Lead students to the anterior and posterior edges of these muscles to feel how they are sandwiched between the soleus and extensor digitorum longus.

TGB, 3rd p. 369-370	Backpack Leg & Foot	Handbook p. 188-189	DVD Leg & Foot

Leg & Foot

Extensors of the Ankle and Toes

Tibialis Anterior

A
- Invert the foot
- Dorsiflex the ankle (talocrural joint)

O Proximal lateral surface of tibia and interosseous membrane

I Medial cuneiform, base of the first metatarsal

N Deep peroneal

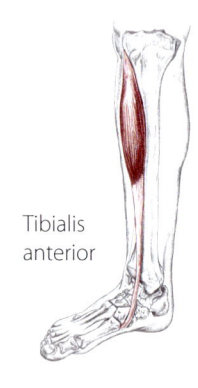

Tibialis anterior

Extensor Digitorum Longus

A
- Extend the second through fifth toes (metatarsophalangeal and interphalangeal joints)
- Dorsiflex the ankle (talocrural joint)
- Evert the foot

O Proximal anterior shaft of fibula and interosseous membrane

I Middle and distal phalanges of second through fifth toes

N Deep peroneal

Extensor digitorum longus

Extensor Hallucis Longus

A
- Extend the first toe (metatarsophalangeal and interphalangeal joints)
- Dorsi flex the ankle (talocrural joint)
- Invert the foot

O Middle anterior surface of fibula and interosseous membrane

I Distal phalange of first toe

N Deep peroneal

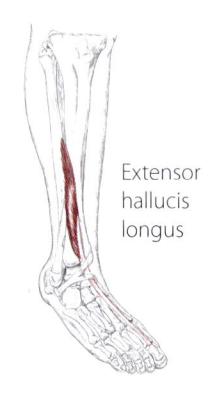

Extensor hallucis longus

Extensors of the Ankle and Toes

Starter Questions
- Which muscle is found just lateral to the shaft of the tibia? *(tibialis anterior)*
- To lengthen the tibialis anterior, how could you position the leg and foot? *(evert the foot, plantar flex the ankle)*
- The four superficial tendons visible on the top of the foot belong to what muscle? *(extensor digitorum longus)*

ADL
- During the swing phase of your gait (lifting the foot after toe-off so that your foot clears the ground)
- Putting on and taking off your socks and shoes
- Wiggling your toes (extensor digitorum and extensor hallucis)

Two Cents
- The extensors "present" very nicely when drawn on the leg.
- Consider pointing out to students how the extensors' muscle bellies "transform" into tendons as the muscles descend down to the ankle and foot.
- Discuss with students how the "stirrup muscles" (tibialis anterior and posterior) create similar and different actions, as well as have common tendinous insertion sites.

TGB, 3rd p. 371-373	Backpack Leg & Foot	Handbook p. 190-191	DVD Leg & Foot

Leg & Foot

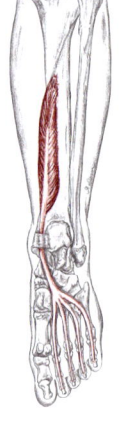

Flexors of the Ankle and Toes

Tibialis Posterior

A
- Invert the foot
- Plantar flex the ankle (talocrural joint)

O Proximal posterior shaft of tibia, proximal fibula and interosseous membrane

I Navicular, cuneiforms, cuboid and bases of second through fourth metatarsals

N Tibial

Tibialis posterior

Flexor Digitorum Longus

A
- Flex the second through fifth toes (metatarsophalangeal and interphalangeal joints)
- Weak plantar flexion of ankle (talocrural joint)
- Invert the foot

O Middle posterior surface of tibia

I Distal phalanges of second through fifth toes

N Tibial

Flexor digitorum longus

Flexor Hallucis Longus

A
- Flex the first toe (metatarsophalangeal and interphalangeal joints)
- Weak plantar flexion of ankle (talocrural joint)
- Invert the foot

O Middle half of posterior fibula

I Distal phalange of first toe

N Tibial

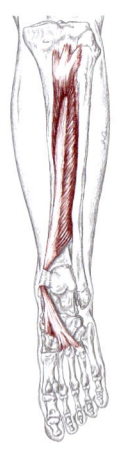

Flexor hallucis longus

Flexors of the Ankle and Toes

Starter Questions
- The distal tendons of the flexors course around the back of what prominent bony landmark? *(medial malleolus)*
- What is the mnemonic device that corresponds to the initials of the tendons and vessels that pass behind the malleolus? *(Tom, Dick AN' Harry)*
- How could you position the ankle to put these muscles in a shortened position? *(invert the foot and plantar flex the ankle)*

ADL
- Balancing on one foot
- Hiking on a rocky trail (small, specific stabilizing movements of the foot)
- Walking on tiptoes
- Turning the hot water tap with your toes when lying in the tub (flexion of the toes with subtle movements of the foot and ankle)

Two Cents
- There's disappointingly little tissue of the flexors to access. With that said, students are often surprised at what they feel in the space between the tibial shaft and the soleus when they ask their partners to wiggle their toes.
- Consider using the mnemonic device "Tom, Dick AN' Harry" to help students remember the order of structures around the medial ankle.

TGB, 3rd p. 374-376	Backpack Leg & Foot	Handbook p. 190-191	DVD Leg & Foot

Muscles of the Foot

Extensor Digitorum Brevis

A Extend the second through fourth toes (metatarsophalangeal and interphalangeal joints)

O Calcaneus (dorsal surface)

I Second through four toes via the extensor digitorum longus tendons

N Deep peroneal

✺ ✺ ✺

Flexor Digitorum Brevis

A Flex middle phalanges of the second through fifth toes (proximal interphalangeal joints)

O Calcaneus (plantar surface)

I Middle phalanges of second through fifth toes

N Medial plantar

✺ ✺ ✺

Abductor Hallucis

A • Abduct the first toe (metatarsophalangeal joint)
 • Assist to flex the first toe (metatarsophalangeal joint)

O Calcaneus (plantar surface)

I Proximal phalange of first toe (medial side) and medial sesamoid bone

N Medial plantar

✺ ✺ ✺

Abductor Digiti Minimi

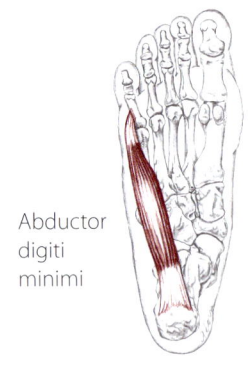

A • Flex the fifth toe
 • Assist to abduct the fifth toe (metatarsophalangeal joint)

O Calcaneus (plantar surface)

I Proximal phalange of fifth toe (lateral side)

N Lateral plantar

Extensor digitorum brevis

Flexor digitorum brevis

Abductor hallucis

Abductor digiti minimi

Muscles of the Foot

Starter Questions
- Looking at the names of the following two muscles, what information can you gather about each of them?

    Flexor Digitorum Brevis   **Abductor Hallucis**

- The most superficial layer of muscles on the foot's plantar surface is comprised of how many muscles and what are their names? *(three; abductor digiti minimi, flexor digitorum brevis, abductor hallucis)*
- What sheet of connective tissue along the foot's plantar surface is superficial to the first layer of muscles? *(plantar aponeurosis)*

ADL
- Stabilization when you are balancing on one foot
- Rock climbing (requires serious work from all of the toes)
- Walking on a patch of ice (notice how your toes suddenly "grab")

Two Cents
- With such long names and lengthy attachment descriptions, consider a game that encourages students to identify information about these muscles.
- Since the plantar muscles are not very discernible, ask students to draw the outlines of the three superficial plantar muscles on one foot and then palpate them on the other foot. This way they have a much better chance of visualizing the bellies' locations.

TGB, 3rd	Backpack	Handbook
p. 377-381	Leg & Foot	p. 190-191

Leg & Foot

Other Structures of the Knee and Leg

	TGB, 3rd ed.
Tibiofemoral Joint	382
Tibiofibular Joints	383
Fibular and Tibial Collateral Ligaments	384
Menisci of the Knee	385
Bursae of the Knee	386
Popliteal Artery	386
Common Peroneal Nerve	387

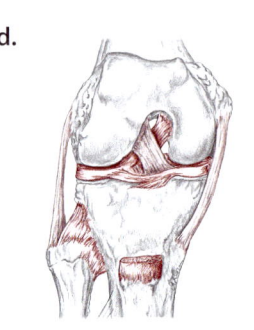

TGB, 3rd p. 382-387	Backpack Leg & Foot	Handbook p. 192-194, 198

Other Structures of the Ankle and Foot

	TGB, 3rd ed.
Talocrural Joint	388
Talotarsal Joints	389
Ligaments of the Foot	389
Deltoid Ligament	391
Plantar Calcaneonavicular (Spring) Ligament	391
Retinacula of the Ankle	392
Plantar Aponeurosis	393
Posterior Tibial Artery	393
Dorsalis Pedis Artery	394
Sesamoid Bones of First Metatarsal	394
Calcaneal Bursae	394

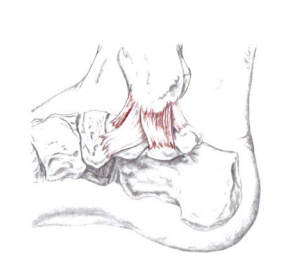

TGB, 3rd p. 388-394	Backpack Leg & Foot	Handbook p. 195-198

NOTES

✦ Synergists - Muscles Working Together

Shoulder (p. 71-73)
(glenohumeral joint)

Flexion
Deltoid (anterior fibers)
Pectoralis major (upper fibers)
Biceps brachii
Coracobrachialis

Extension
Deltoid (posterior fibers)
Latissimus dorsi
Teres major
Infraspinatus
Teres minor
Pectoralis major (lower fibers)
Triceps brachii (long head)

Horizontal Abduction
Deltoid (posterior fibers)
Infraspinatus
Teres minor

Horizontal Adduction
Deltoid (anterior fibers)
Pectoralis major (upper fibers)

Abduction
Deltoid (all fibers)
Supraspinatus

Adduction
Latissimus dorsi
Teres major
Infraspinatus
Teres minor
Pectoralis major (all fibers)
Triceps brachii (long head)
Coracobrachialis

Lateral Rotation (external rotation)
Deltoid (posterior fibers)
Infraspinatus
Teres minor

Medial Rotation (internal rotation)
Deltoid (anterior fibers)
Latissimus dorsi
Teres major
Subscapularis
Pectoralis major (all fibers)

Scapula (p. 73-74)
(scapulothoracic joint)

Elevation
Trapezius (upper fibers)
Rhomboid major
Rhomboid minor
Levator scapula

Depression
Trapezius (lower fibers)
Serratus anterior (with the origin fixed)
Pectoralis minor

Adduction (retraction)
Trapezius (middle fibers)
Rhomboid major
Rhomboid minor

Abduction (protraction)
Serratus anterior (with the origin fixed)
Pectoralis minor

Upward Rotation
Trapezius (upper and lower fibers)

Downward Rotation
Rhomboid major
Rhomboid minor
Levator scapula

Elbow (p. 138)
(humeroulnar and humeroradial joints)

Flexion
Biceps brachii
Brachialis
Brachioradialis
Flexor carpi radialis
Flexor carpi ulnaris (assists)
Palmaris longus
Pronator teres (assists)
Extensor carpi radialis longus (assists)
Extensor carpi radialis brevis (assists)

Extension
Triceps brachii (all heads)
Anconeus

Forearm (p. 138)
(proximal and distal radioulnar joints)

Supination
Biceps brachii
Supinator
Brachioradialis (assists)

Pronation
Pronator teres
Pronator quadratus
Brachioradialis (assists)

Wrist (p. 138-139)
(radiocarpal joint)

Extension
Extensor carpi radialis longus
Extensor carpi radialis brevis
Extensor carpi ulnaris
Extensor digitorum (assists)

Flexion
Flexor carpi radialis
Flexor carpi ulnaris
Palmaris longus
Flexor digitorum superficialis
Flexor digitorum profundus (assists)

Abduction (radial deviation)
Extensor carpi radialis longus
Extensor carpi radialis brevis
Flexor carpi radialis

Adduction (ulnar deviation)
Extensor carpi ulnaris
Flexor carpi ulnaris

Hand and Fingers (p. 139)
(metacarpophalangeal, proximal and distal interphalangeal joints)

Flexion of the second through fifth fingers
Flexor digitorum superficialis
Flexor digitorum profundus
Flexor digiti minimi brevis (5th)
Lumbricals
Dorsal interossei (2nd - 4th) (assists)
Palmar interossei (2nd, 4th, 5th) (assists)

Extension of the second through fifth fingers
Extensor digitorum
Extensor indicis (2nd)
Lumbricals
Dorsal interossei (2nd - 4th) (assists)
Palmar interossei (2nd, 4th, 5th) (assists)

Abduction of the second through fifth fingers
Dorsal interossei (2nd - 4th)
Abductor digiti minimi (5th)

Adduction of the second through fifth fingers
Palmar interossei (2nd, 4th, 5th)
Extensor indicis (2nd) (assists)

Opposition of the fifth finger
Opponens digiti minimi
Abductor digiti minimi (assists)
Flexor digiti minimi brevis (assists)

Thumb (p. 139)
(first carpometacarpal and metacarpophalangeal joints)

Flexion
Flexor pollicis longus
Flexor pollicis brevis
Adductor pollicis (assists)
Palmar interossei (1st) (assists)

Extension
Extensor pollicis longus
Extensor pollicis brevis
Abductor pollicis longus
Palmar interossei (1st) (assists)

Abduction
Abductor pollicis longus
Abductor pollicis brevis

Adduction
Adductor pollicis
Palmar interossei (1st)

Opposition
Opponens pollicis
Flexor pollicis brevis (assists)
Abductor pollicis brevis (assists)

Vertebral Column (p. 200-201)

Flexion
Rectus abdominis
External oblique (bilaterally)
Internal oblique (bilaterally)

Extension
Spinalis (bilaterally)
Longissimus (bilaterally)
Iliocostalis (bilaterally)
Multifidi (bilaterally)
Rotatores (bilaterally)
Semispinalis capitis
Quadratus lumborum (assists)
Intertransversarii (bilaterally)
Interspinalis
Latissimus dorsi (when arm is fixed, p. 79)

Rotation (all unilaterally)
Multifidi (to the opposite side)
Rotatores (to the opposite side)
External oblique (to the opposite side)
Internal oblique (to the same side)

Lateral Flexion
   (unilaterally to the **same** side)
Spinalis
Longissimus
Iliocostalis
Quadratus lumborum
External oblique
Internal oblique
Intertransversarii
Latissimus dorsi (p. 79)

Ribs/Thorax (p. 201)

Elevation/Expansion
Anterior scalene (bilaterally)
Middle scalene (bilaterally)
Posterior scalene (bilaterally)
Sternocleidomastoid (assists)
External intercostals (assists)
Serratus posterior superior
Pectoralis major
   (may assist if arm is fixed)
Pectoralis minor (if scapula is fixed)
Serratus anterior (if scapula is fixed)
Subclavius (first rib)

Depression/Collapse
Internal intercostals (assists)
Serratus posterior inferior

Muscles of Inhalation
Diaphragm
Anterior scalene (bilaterally)
Middle scalene (bilaterally)
Posterior scalene (bilaterally)
Sternocleidomastoid (assist)
External intercostals (assists)
Serratus posterior superior
Quadratus lumborum
Pectoralis major (assist if arm is fixed)
Pectoralis minor (if scapula is fixed)
Serratus anterior (if scapula is fixed)
Subclavius (first rib)

Muscles of Exhalation
Internal intercostals (assists)
Serratus posterior inferior
External oblique
  (by compressing abdominal contents)
Internal oblique
  (by compressing abdominal contents)
Transverse abdominis
  (by compressing abdominal contents)
Quadratus lumborum

Cervical Spine (p. 248-249)

Flexion
Sternocleidomastoid (bilaterally)
Anterior scalene (bilaterally)
Longus capitis (bilaterally)
Longus colli (bilaterally)

Extension
Trapezius - upper fibers (bilaterally)
Levator scapula (bilaterally)
Splenius capitis (bilaterally)
Splenius cervicis (bilaterally)
Rectus capitis posterior major
Rectus capitis posterior minor
Oblique capitis superior
Semispinalis capitis
Longissimus capitis (assists, p. 202)
Longissimus cervicis (assists, p. 202)
Iliocostalis cervicis (assists, p. 202)

Rotation
  (unilaterally to the **same** side)
Levator scapula
Splenius capitis
Splenius cervicis
Rectus capitis posterior major
Oblique capitis inferior
Longus colli
Longus capitis
Longissimus capitis (assists, p. 202)
Longissimus cervicis (assists, p. 202)
Iliocostalis cervicis (assists, p. 202)

Rotation
  (unilaterally to the **opposite** side)
Trapezius (upper fibers)
Sternocleidomastoid
Anterior scalene
Middle scalene
Posterior scalene

Lateral Flexion
  (unilaterally to the **same** side)
Trapezius (upper fibers)
Levator scapula
Splenius capitis
Splenius cervicis
Sternocleidomastoid
Longus capitis
Longus colli
Anterior scalene (with ribs fixed)
Middle scalene (with ribs fixed)
Posterior scalene (with ribs fixed)
Longissimus capitis (assists, p. 202)
Longissimus cervicis (assists, p. 202)
Iliocostalis cervicis (assists, p. 202)

Mandible (p. 249)
(temporomandibular joint)

Elevation
Masseter
Temporalis
Medial pterygoid

Depression
Geniohyoid
Mylohyoid
Stylohyoid
Digastric (with hyoid bone fixed)
Platysma (assists)

Protraction
Lateral pterygoid (bilaterally)
Medial pterygoid (bilaterally)

Retraction
Temporalis
Digastric

Lateral Deviation (unilaterally)
Lateral pterygoid (to the opposite side)
Medial pterygoid (to the opposite side)

Pelvis

Anterior Tilt (downward rotation)
Latissimus dorsi (assists, p. 79)

Posterior Tilt (upward rotation)
Biceps femoris
Semitendinosus
Semimembranosus
Psoas minor

Lateral Tilt (elevation)
Quadratus lumborum
Latissimus dorsi (assists, p. 79)

Coxal (p. 296-298)
(hip joint)

Flexion
Rectus femoris
Gluteus medius (anterior fibers)
Gluteus minimus
Adductor magnus (assists)
Adductor longus (assists)
Adductor brevis (assists)
Pectineus (assists)
Tensor fasciae latae
Sartorius
Psoas major
Iliacus

Extension
Biceps femoris
Semitendinosus
Semimembranosus
Gluteus maximus (all fibers)
Gluteus medius (posterior fibers)
Adductor magnus (posterior fibers)

Medial Rotation (internal rotation)
Semitendinosus
Semimembranosus
Gluteus medius (anterior fibers)
Gluteus minimus
Adductor magnus
Adductor longus
Adductor brevis
Gracilis
Pectineus
Tensor fasciae latae

Lateral Rotation (external rotation)
Biceps femoris
Gluteus maximus (all fibers)
Gluteus medius (posterior fibers)
Sartorius
Piriformis
Quadratus femoris
Obturator internus
Obturator externus
Gemellus superior
Gemellus inferior
Psoas major
Iliacus

Abduction
Gluteus maximus (all fibers)
Gluteus medius (all fibers)
Gluteus minimus
Tensor fasciae latae
Sartorius
Piriformis (when the hip is flexed)

Adduction
Adductor magnus
Adductor longus
Adductor brevis
Pectineus
Gracilis
Psoas major
Iliacus
Gluteus maximus (lower fibers)

Knee (p. 299)
(tibiofemoral joint)

Flexion
Biceps femoris
Semitendinosus
Semimembranosus
Gracilis
Sartorius
Gastrocnemius
Popliteus
Plantaris (weak)

Extension
Rectus femoris
Vastus lateralis
Vastus medialis
Vastus intermedius

Medial Rotation of Flexed Knee
Semitendinosus
Semimembranosus
Gracilis
Sartorius
Popliteus

Lateral Rotation of Flexed Knee
Biceps femoris

Ankle (p. 362)
(talocrural joint)

Plantar Flexion
Gastrocnemius
Soleus
Tibialis posterior
Peroneus longus (assists)
Peroneus brevis (assists)
Flexor digitorum longus (weak)
Flexor hallucis longus (weak)
Plantaris (weak)

Dorsiflexion
Tibialis anterior
Extensor digitorum longus
Extensor hallucis longus

Foot and Toes (p. 363)
(talotarsal,
midtarsal,
tarsometatarsal,
metatarsophalangeal,
proximal and distal
interphalangeal joints)

Inversion
Tibialis anterior
Tibialis posterior
Flexor digitorum longus
Flexor hallucis longus
Extensor hallucis longus

Eversion
Peroneus longus
Peroneus brevis
Extensor digitorum longus

**Flexion of Second
through Fifth Toes**
Flexor digitorum longus
Flexor digitorum brevis
Lumbricals
Quadratus plantae (assists)
Dorsal interossei (2nd - 4th)
Plantar interossei (3rd - 5th)
Abductor digiti minimi (5th)
Flexor digiti minimi (5th)

**Extension of Second
through Fifth Toes**
Extensor digitorum longus
Extensor digitorum brevis (2nd - 4th)
Lumbricals

**Adduction of Second
through Fifth Toes**
Plantar interossei (3rd - 5th)

**Abduction of Second
through Fifth Toes**
Dorsal interossei (2nd - 4th)
Abductor digiti minimi (5th) (assists)

Flexion of First Toe
Flexor hallucis longus
Flexor hallucis brevis
Abductor hallucis (assists)

Extension of First Toe
Extensor hallucis longus
Extensor hallucis brevis

Adduction of First Toe
Adductor hallucis

Abduction of First Toe
Abductor hallucis

Glossary of Terms

abdomen - the region between the diaphragm and the pelvis

acetabulum - the rounded cavity on the external surface of the coxal bone; the head of the femur articulates with the acetabulum to form the coxal joint

adhesion - abnormal adherence of collagen fibers to surrounding structures during immobilization, following trauma or as a complication of surgery, which restricts normal elasticity of the structures involved

anatomical position - erect posture with face forward, arms at sides, forearms supinated (so that palms of the hands face forward) and fingers and thumbs in extension

antagonist - a muscle that performs the opposite action of the prime mover and synergist muscles

antecubital - the anterior side of the elbow

anterior - toward the front or ventral surface

anterior tilt of pelvis - tilt in which the vertical plane through the anterior superior iliac spines (ASISes) are anterior to the vertical plane through the symphysis pubis

appendage - a structure attached to the body such as the upper and lower extremities

arm - the portion of the upper limb between the shoulder and elbow joints

arthrology - the study of joints

articular facet - a small articular surface of a bone, especially a vertebra

articular process - a small flat projection found on the surfaces of the arches of the vertebrae on either side incorporating the articular surface

articulation - a joint or connection of bones

atlas - first cervical vertebra, articulating with the occipital bone and rotating around the odontoid process of the axis

axis - the second cervical vertebra

bilateral - pertaining to two sides

bursa - a small, fluid-filled sack that reduces friction between two structures

cartilaginous joint - a joint in which two bony surfaces are united by cartilage; the two types of cartilaginous joints are **synchondroses** and **symphyses**

caudal - downward, away from the head (toward the tail)

cephalic - toward the head

collagen - the protein of connective tissue fibers

concentric contraction - a shortening of the muscle during a contraction; a type of isotonic exercise

condyle - a rounded articular surface at the extremity of a bone

connective tissue - the supportive tissues of the body, made of ground substance and fibrous tissues, taking a wide variety of forms

contraction - an increase in muscle tension, with or without change in overall length

Glossary of Terms

coronal - a vertical plane perpendicular to the sagittal plane dividing the body into anterior and posterior portions, also called the frontal plane

coronal axis - a horizontal line extending from side to side, around which the movements of flexion and extension take place

cramp - a spasmodic contraction of one or many muscles

cranial - upward, toward the head

crepitation - an audible and/or palpable crunching during movement of tendons or ligaments over bone

cutaneous - referring to the skin

deep - away from the surface of the body; the opposite of superficial

distal - farther from the center or median line or from the thorax

dorsal - relating to the back; posterior

eccentric muscle contraction - an overall lengthening of the muscle while it is contracting or resisting a workload

edema - a local or generalized condition in which body tissues contain an excessive amount of fluid

facet - a small plane or concave surface

fascia - a general term for a layer or layers of loose or dense fibrous connective tissue

fascicle - a bundle of muscle fibers

fibrous joint - a joint in which the components are connected by fibrous tissue

flexibility - the ability to readily adapt to changes in position or alignment; may be expressed as normal, limited, or excessive

forearm - the portion of the upper limb between the elbow and wrist joints

frontal plane - a vertical plane perpendicular to the sagittal plane dividing the body into anterior and posterior portions, also called the coronal plane

genu valgum - "knock-knees," defined as a lateral displacement of the distal end of the distal bone in the joint

genu varum - "bowlegs," defined as a medial displacement of the distal end of the distal bone in the joint

impingement - an encroachment on the space occupied by soft tissue, such as nerve or muscle

inferior - away from the head

insertion - the more mobile attachment site of a muscle to a bone; the opposite end is the origin

interstitial - the space within an organ or tissue

interstitial fluid - the fluid that surrounds cells

isometric - increase in tension without change in muscle length

isotonic - increase in tension with change in muscle length (in the direction of shortening); concentric contraction

isotonic contraction (dynamic) - a concentric or eccentric contraction of a muscle; a muscle contraction performed with movement

Index 139

Glossary of Terms

kinesiology - the study of movement

kyphosis - a condition characterized by an abnormally increased convexity in the curvature of the thoracic spine as viewed from the side

lateral - away from the midline

lateral tilt - pelvic tilt in which the crest of the ilium is higher on one side than on the other

leg - the portion of the lower extremity between the knee and ankle joints

ligament - a fibrous connective tissue that connects bone to bone

longitudinal axis - a vertical line extending in a cranial/caudal direction about which movements of rotation take place

lordosis - an abnormally increased concavity in the curvature of the lumbar spine as viewed from the side

lymph node - a small oval structure located along lymphatic vessels

lymphatic - pertains to the system of vessels involved with drainage of bodily fluids (lymph)

medial - toward the midline

muscle - an organ composed of one of three types of muscle tissue (skeletal, cardiac or visceral), specialized for contraction

muscle contracture - an increase of tension in the muscle caused by activation of the contractile mechanism of the muscle

myofascial - pertains to skeletal muscles ensheathed by fibrous connective tissue

occipital condyles - elongated oval facets on the undersurface of the occipital bone on either side of the foramen magnum, which articulate with the atlas vertebra

odontoid process (or dens) - a process projecting upward from the body of the the axis vertebra around which the atlas rotates

origin - the more stationary attachment site of a muscle to a bone; the opposite end is the insertion

palmar - toward the palm

palpable - touchable, accessible

palpate - to examine or explore by touching (an organ or area of the body), usually as a diagnostic aid

paravertebrals - alongside or near the vertebral column

pelvic girdle - the two hip bones

pelvic tilt - an anterior (forward), a posterior (backward) or a lateral (vertical) tilt of the pelvis from neutral position

pelvis - composed of the two hip bones, sacrum and coccyx

periosteum - the fibrous connective tissue which surrounds the surface of bones

posterior - toward the back or dorsal surface

posterior tilt of pelvis - tilt in which the vertical plane through the anterior superior iliac spines (ASISes) are posterior to the vertical plane through the symphysis pubis

Glossary of Terms

prime mover - a muscle that carries out an action

process - a projection or outgrowth from a bone

proximal - nearer to the center or midline of the body

range of motion - the range, usually expressed in degrees, through which a joint can move or be moved

range of motion, active - the free movement across any joint of moving levers that is produced by contracting muscles

range of motion, passive - the free movement that is produced by external forces across any joint or moving levers

retinaculum - a network, usually pertaining to a band of connective tissue

sagittal axis - a horizontal line extending from front to back, about which movements of abduction and adduction take place

sagittal plane - a plane that divides the body into left and right portions

soft tissue - usually referring to myofascial tissues, or any tissues which do not contain minerals (such as bone)

superficial - nearer to the surface of the body; the opposite of deep

superior - toward the head

surface anatomy - the study of structures that can be identified from the outside of the body

symphysis - a union between two bones formed by fibrocartilage

synchondrosis - a union between two bones formed either by hyaline cartilage or fibrocartilage

synergist - a muscle that supports the prime mover

synovial joint - a joint containing a lubricating substance (synovial fluid) and lined with a synovial membrane or capsule

tactile - pertaining to touch

tendon - a fibrous tissue connecting skeletal muscle to bone

thigh - the portion of the lower extremity between the coxal and knee joints

thorax - the region between the neck and abdomen

tightness - shortness; denotes a slight to moderate decrease in muscle length; movement in the direction of lengthening the muscle is limited

transverse plane - a plane that divides the body into superior and inferior (or proximal and distal) portions

trunk - the part of the body to which the upper and lower extremities attach

unilateral - pertaining to one side

ventral - a synonym for anterior, usually applied to the torso

Pronunciation and Etymology

etymology   **et**-i-**mol**-o-gee   the science of the origin and development of a word

ab- (as in abduct)		L. away from
abdomen	**ab**-do-men	L. belly
abdominis	ab-**dah**-min-is	
abduct	**ab**-duct	L. to lead away, bring apart
acetabulum	as-e-**tab**-u-lum	L. a little saucer for vinegar
acromioclavicular	a-**kro**-me-o-kla-**vik**-u-lar	
acromion	a-**cro**-me-on	Grk. *akron*, top + *omos*, shoulder
ad- (as in adduct)		L. toward
adduct	**ad**-duct	L. to bring together
adipose	a-di-**pose**	L. fat, copious
alar	**ay**-lar	
anconeus	an-**ko**-nee-us	Grk. elbow
annular	**an**-u-ler	L. ringlike
annulus	**an**-u-lus	L. ring
aponeurosis	**ap**-o-nu-**ro**-sis	Grk. *apo*, from + *neuron*, nerve or tendon
appendicular	ap-en-**dik**-u-lar	L. to hang to
arrector pili	a-rek-tor **pee**-li	L. *arrector*, lifter; *pilus*, hair
artery	**ar**-ter-e	Grk. windpipe
atlantoaxial	at-**lan**-to-**ak**-se-al	
atlantooccipital	at-**lan**-to-ok-**si**-pi-tal	
axial	**ak**-see-al	L. axle
axilla	**ak**-sil-a	L. armpit
axillary	**ak**-si-**lar**-ee	
basilic	bah-**sil**-ic	Arabic *basilik*, inner
biceps	**bi**-seps	L. *bis*, twice + *caput*, head
biceps brachii	**bi**-seps **bray**-key-i	L. two-headed muscle of the arm

142   **Instructor's Field Guide**   Grk.   Greek   Fr.   French
                                                L.   Latin   AS.   Anglo-Saxon

Pronunciation and Etymology

biceps femoris	**bi**-seps fe-**mor**-is	Grk. the two-headed (muscle) of the thigh
brachial	**bray**-key-al	L. relating to the arm
brachialis	**bray**-key-**al**-is	
brachii	**bray**-key-i	L. of the arm
brachioradialis	**bray**-key-o-**ra**-de-**a**-lis	
brevis	**breh**-vis	L. short
bursa	**bur**-sah	L. a purse
calcaneocuboid	kal-**ka**-ne-o-**ku**-boyd	
calcaneofibular	kal-**ka**-ne-o-**fib**-u-lar	
calcaneus	kal-**kay**-nee-us	L. heel
capillary	**kap**-i-**lar**-ee	L. hairlike
capitate	**kap**-i-tate	L. head-shaped
capitis	**kap**-i-tis	L. of the head
capitulum	ka-**pit**-u-lum	L. small head
carotid	ka-**rot**-id	Grk. causing deep sleep
carpal	**kar**-pul	Grk. pertaining to the wrist
carpi	**kar**-pi	L. of the wrist
cartilage	**kar**-ti-lij	L. gristle
cauda equina	**kaw**-da eh-**kwy**-na	L. horse's tail
cephalic	se-**fa**-lic	Grk. pertaining to the head
cervical	**ser**-vi-kal	L. referring to the neck
cervicis	**ser**-vi-sis	L. neck
chest		AS. box
cisterna chyli	sis-**turn**-a **ki**-lee	
clavicle	**klav**-i-k'l	L. little key
coccyx	**kok**-siks	Grk. cuckoo
collateral	ko-**lat**-er-al	L. of both sides
condyle	**kon**-dial	Grk. knuckle
conoid	**ko**-noid	Grk. cone-shaped
coracoacromial	**kor**-a-**ko**-a-**cro**-mi-ul	

Index 143

Pronunciation and Etymology

coracobrachialis	**kor**-a-ko-**bra**-kee-**al**-is	
coracoclavicular	**kor**-a-**ko**-cla-**vic**-u-lar	
coracoid	**kor**-a-koyd	Grk. raven's beak
coronal	ko-**ro**-nal	L. crownlike
coronoid	**kor**-a-noyd	Grk. crown-shaped
costal	**kos**-tal	L. rib
coxal	**kox**-sal	L. hip
cranio-	**cra**-nee-o	Grk. skull
cranium	**cra**-nium	Grk. skull
cremaster	kre-**mas**-ter	L. to suspend
cricoid	**kri**-koyd	Grk. ring-shaped
cruciate	**kroo**-she-at	L. cross-shaped
cuboid	**ku**-boyd	Grk. cube-shaped
cuboideonavicular	**ku**-boyd-e-o-na-**vik**-u-lar	
cuneiform	ku-**ne**-i-form	L. wedge-shaped
deltoid	**del**-toid	Grk. *delta*, capital letter D (Δ) in the Greek alphabet
diaphragm	**di**-a-**fram**	Grk. a partition, wall
digastric	di-**gas**-trik	Grk. double-bellied
digit	**di**-jit	L. finger
digitigrade	**di**-ji-tah-grade	L. toe-walking
dorsalis pedis	**dor**-sal-is **peh**-dis	L. *dorsum*, back; *pedis*, foot
dorsi	**dor**-si	L. of the back
dura mater	**dyoo**-ra **ma**-ter	L. tough mother
epi-	**eh**-pee	Grk. above, upon
facet	**fac**-et	Fr. small face
facial	**fa**-shal	L. pertaining to the face
fascia	**fash**-ah	L. a band, bandage
fasciae	**fash**-ay	plural for fascia
fascicle	**fas**-i-kl	L. little bundle
femur	**fee**-mur	L. thigh

Pronunciation and Etymology

fibula	**fib**-u-la	L. pin or buckle
flavum	**flay**-vum	
flex		L. to bend
foot		AS. *fot*
foramen	for-**ay**-men	L. a passage or opening
fossa	**fos**-a	L. a shallow depression
furcula	**fur**-ku-la	L. a little fork
gastrocnemius	gas-trok-**ne**-me-us	Grk. *gaster*, stomach + *kneme*, leg
gemellus	jem-**el**-us	L. twins
geniohyoid	je-ne-o-**hi**-oyd	Grk. *genion*, chin
genu valgum	je-noo **val**-gum	
genu varum	je-noo **va**-rum	
gland		L. acorn
glenoid	**glen**-oid	Grk. eyeball
glossus	**glah**-sis	Grk. tongue
gluteus	**gloo**-te-us	Grk. *gloutos*, buttocks
gracilis	gra-**cil**-is	L. slender, graceful
hallucis	**hal**-ah-sis	
hallux	**hal**-uks	L. first toe
ham		AS. haunch
hamate	**ham**-ate	L. hooked
hamulus	**ham**-u-lus	L. a small hook
humerus	**hu**-mer-us	L. upper arm
hyoid	**hi**-oyd	Grk. U-shaped
hypothenar	**hi**-po-**thee**-nar	Grk. *hypo*, under or below
iliacus	i-**lee**-a-cus	L. pertaining to the loin
iliocostalis	il-ee-o-kos-**ta**-lis	L. from hip to rib
ilium	**il**-ee-um	L. groin, flank
indicis	**in**-di-kis	
inferior	in-**fe**-ree-or	L. below

Index 145

Pronunciation and Etymology

infraspinatus	**in**-fra-spi-**na**-tus	
inguinal	**ing**-gwi-nal	L. of the groin
interdigitate	in-ter-**dij**-i-tate	L. to interlock, as fingers of clasped hands
interroseus	in-ter-**ah**-see-us	L. between bones
interspinalis	in-ter-spi-**na**-lis	
interstitial	in-ter-**stish**-al	L. placed between
intertransverserii	in-ter-trans-**verse**-er-**i**	
intertubercular	**in**-tur-tu-**ber**-ku-lar	
ischiocavernosus	**ish**-she-o-**ka**-ver-**no**-sus	
ischium	**ish**-ee-um	Grk. hip
jaw		ME. iawe
joint		L. to join
jugular	**jug**-u-lar	L. throat
kyphosis	ki-**fo**-sis	Grk. bent, curved, or stooped
labrum	**lay**-brum	L. lip
lamina	**lam**-i-na	L. thin plate, leaf
latae	**la**-ta	L. broad
lateral	**lat**-er-al	L. to the side
latissimus dorsi	la-**tis**-i-mus **dor**-si	L. widest of the back
levator	leh-**va**-tor	L. lifter
levator scapula	leh-**va**-tor **skap**-u-la	
ligament	**lig**-a-ment	L. a band
linea aspera	**lin**-e-a **as**-per-a	L. rough line
longissimus	lon-**jis**-i-mus	L. longest
longus colli	**long**-us **ko**-li	L. long (muscle) of the neck
lordosis	lor-**doh**-sis	Grk. bent backward
lumbar	**lum**-bar	L. loin
lumborum	lum-**bor**-um	
lumbrical	**lum**-bri-kal	L. earthworm
lunate	**lu**-nate	L. crescent-shaped

Pronunciation and Etymology

lymph	limf	L. pure spring water
magnus	**mag**-nus	L. large
malleolus	mal-e-**o**-lus	L. little hammer
mandible	**man**-di-ble	L. lower jawbone
manubrium	ma-**nu**-bree-um	L. handle
masseter	**mas**-se-ter	Grk. chewer
mastoid	**mas**-toyd	Grk. breast-shaped
maxilla	**max**-il-a	L. jawbone
medial	**me**-dee-ul	L. middle
menisci	men-**is**-ki	plural for meniscus
meniscofemoral	men-**is**-ko-fem-**or**-al	
meniscus	men-**is**-kus	Grk. crescent-shaped
menisci	men-**is**-ki	plural for meniscus
mentalis	men-**tal**-is	L. chin
meta-	**met**-a	Grk. after or beyond
metacarpal	met-a-**kar**-pul	
metacarpophalangeal	met-a-**kar**-po-fa-**lan**-jee-al	
metatarsal	met-a-**tar**-sal	
metatarsophalangeal	met-a-**tar**-so-fa-lan-**jee**-al	
minimi	**min**-i-mee	L. smallest
multifidi	mul-**tif**-i-di	L. *fidi*, to split
muscle	**mus**-el	L. *musculus*, a little mouse
mylohyoid	**my**-lo-**hi**-oyd	Grk. *myle*, mill
myo-		Grk. muscle
nape		ME. back of the neck
nasal	**na**-zl	L. nose
navicular	na-**vik**-u-lar	L. boat-shaped
neck		AS. nape
nerve		L. sinew
nuchae	**nu**-kay	L. nape of neck

Index 147

Pronunciation and Etymology

nuchal	**nu**-kal	L. back of the neck
oblique	o-**bleek**	L. diagonal, slanted
obturator	**ob**-tu-**ra**-tor	L. obstructor
occipitofrontalis	ok-**sip**-i-to-fron-**ta**-lis	
occiput	**ok**-si-put	L. the back of skull
odontoid	o-**don**-toyd	Grk. toothlike
olecranon	o-**lek**-ran-on	Grk. elbow
omohyoid	**o**-mo-**hi**-oyd	Grk. *omos*, shoulder
opponens	o-**po**-nens	L. opposing
palpate	**pal**-pate	L. *palpare*, to touch
panniculus carnosus	pan-**ik**-u-lus car-**no**-sis	L. small, fleshy garment
parietal	puh-**ri**′e-tul	L. wall
parotid	pa-**rot**-id	Grk. beside the ear
patella	pa-**tel**-a	L. small pan
pectineus	pek-**tin**-e-us	L. comblike
pectoralis	**pek**-to-**ra**-lis	L. chest
pedicle	**ped**-i-k′l	L. a little foot
pelvis	**pel**-vis	L. basin
penis		L. tail
peroneus	per-**o**-ne-us	Grk. pin, buckle
pes anserinus	pes **an**-ser-**i**-nus	L. *pedis*, foot; L. *anserinus*, gooselike
phalange	fa-**lan**-jee	Grk. closely knit row, line of battle
phalanx	**fal**-anks	singular for phalange
piriformis	pir-i-**form**-is	L. pear-shaped
pisiform	**pi**-si-form	L. pea-shaped
plantar	**plan**-tar	L. the sole of the foot
plantaris	plan-**tar**-is	Fr. pertaining to the sole of the foot
plantigrade	**plant**-i-grad	L. sole-walking
platysma	pla-**tiz**-ma	Grk. plate
plexus	**plek**-sus	L. interwoven

Pronunciation and Etymology

pollex	**pol**-eks	L. thumb
pollicis	**pol**-li-sis	L. thumb
popliteus	pop-**lit**-e-us	L. ham of the knee
process	**pros**-es	L. going forth
profundus	pro-**fun**-dus	L. deep
pronate	**pro**-nate	L. bent forward
psoas	**so**-as	Grk. muscle of the loin
pterygoid	ter-i-**goyd**	Grk. wing shaped
pubis	**pu**-bis	NL. bone of the groin
quadratus	**kwod**-rait-us	L. squared, four-sided
quadratus lumborum	**kwod**-rait-us lum-**bor**-um	L. four-sided muscle of the lumbar region
quadriceps	**kwod**-ri-seps	L. four-headed
quadruped		Grk. four-footed
radiocapitate	**ray**-dee-o-**kap**-i-tate	
radioscapholunate	**ray**-dee-o-**skaf**-o-**loo**-nate	
radiotriquetrum	**ray**-dee-o-tri-**kwe**-trum	
radius	**ray**-dee-us	L. staff, spoke of a wheel
ramus	**ray**-mus	L. branch
rectus	**rek**-tus	L. straight
retinacula	**ret**-i-**nak**-u-la	plural for retinaculum
retinaculum	**ret**-i-**nak**-u-lum	L. halter, band, rope
retinacula	**ret**-i-**nak**-u-la	plural for retinaculum
rhomboid	**rom**-boyd	Grk. geometry, a parallelogram with oblique angles and only the opposite sides equal
rotatores	ro-ta-**tor**-ays	L. plural for rotators
sacrococcygeal	sa-kro-kok-**sij**-e-al	
sacrotuberous	sa-kro-**tu**-ber-us	
sacrum	**sa**-krum	L. sacred or holy thing, from the use of the sacrum in Roman animal sacrifice
sagittal	**saj**-i-tal	L. arrowlike

Pronunciation and Etymology

saphenous	**sa**-fe-nus	Grk. *saphen*, clearly visible
sartorius	sar-**tor**-ee-us	L. tailor
scalene	**skay**-leen	Grk. uneven
scaphoid	**skaf**-oyd	L. boat-shaped
scapula	**skap**-u-la	L. shoulder, blade
scapulae	**skap**-u-lay	plural for scapula
sciatic	si-**at**-ik	Grk. *ischion*, hip joint
sciatica	si-**at**-ika	L. suffering in the hip
semimembranosus	**sem**-eye-**mem**-bra-**no**-sus	L. half membranous
semispinalis	**sem**-eye-spi-**na**-lis	L. half spinal
semitendinosus	**sem**-eye-**ten**-di-**no**-sus	L. half tendinous
septa	**sep**-ta	plural for septum
septum	**sep**-tum	L. enclosure
septa	**sep**-ta	plural for septum
serratus	ser-**a**-tus	L. notched
sesamoid	**ses**-a-moyd	L. resembling a sesame seed
skeleton	**skel**-et-on	Grk. dried up
skull		ME. bow
soleus	so-**lay**-us	L. *solea*, as in a sole fish
sphenoid	**sfe**-noyd	Grk. wedge-shaped
spinalis capitis	**spi**-na-lis **kap**-i-tis	
spinalis cervicis	**spi**-na-lis **ser**-vi-sis	
spine		L. thorn
splenius	**sple**-nee-us	Grk. bandage
splenius capitis	**sple**-nee-us **kap**-i-tis	L. bandage-like (muscle) of the head
splenius cervicis	**sple**-nee-us **ser**-vi-sis	
stapedius	sta-**pe**-de-us	L. stirrup
sternoclavicular	**ster**-no-kla-**vik**-u-lar	
sternocleidomastoid	**ster**-no-**kli**-do-**mas**-toyd	

150 Instructor's Field Guide

Pronunciation and Etymology

sternohyoid	**ster**-no-**hi**-oyd	
sternothyroid	**ster**-no-**thi**-royd	
sternum	**ster**-num	Grk. chest
stylohyoid	**sti**-lo-**hi**-oyd	
styloid	**sti**-loyd	Grk. a pillar
subclavius	sub-**klay**-vee-us	
subscapularis	sub-**skap**-u-**lar**-is	
superficialis	soo-per-**fish**-ee-**a**-lis	L. on the surface
supinate	**su**-pi-nate	L. bent backward
supraspinatus	soo-pra-spi-**na**-tus	
sustentaculum	sus-ten-**tak**-u-lum	L. support
suture	**su**-chur	L. a seam
symphysis	**sim**-fi-sis	Grk. growing together
synchondrosis	**sin**-con-**dro**-sis	
synovial	sin-**o**-ve-al	L. *synovia*, joint fluid
talocalcaneal	ta-lo-kal-**ka**-ne-al	
talocrural	ta-lo-**kroo**-ral	L. ankle + *crus*, leg
talofibular	ta-lo-**fib**-u-lar	
talonavicular	ta-lo-na-**vik**-u-lar	
talus	**ta**-lus	L. ankle
tarsal	**tar**-sul	Grk. wicker basket
temporalis	tem-po-**ra**-lis	L. time, seen by the graying of hairs in this region
tendon	**ten**-dun	L. to stretch
tensor	**ten**-sor	L. a stretcher
teres	**teh**-reez	L. rounded, finely shaped
tertius	**ter**-she-us	L. third
thenar	**thee**-nar	Grk. palm, flat of the hand
thoracic	tho-**ras**-ik	Grk. chest
thoracolumbar	tho-**rak**-o-**lum**-bar	
thorax	**tho**-raks	Grk. chest

Index 151

Pronunciation and Etymology

thyrohyoid	**thi**-ro-**hi**-oyd	
thyroid	**thi**-royd	Grk. shield
tibia	**tib**-e-a	L. shinbone
trachea	**tray**-ke-a	Grk. rough
tract		L. extent, drawn out
transverse	**trans**-verse	L. across, turned across
trapezium	tra-**pee**-ze-um	Grk. little table
trapezius	tra-**pee**-ze-us	Grk. a little table or trapezoid shape
trapezoid	**trap**-e-zoid	Grk. table-shaped
triceps brachii	**tri**-seps **bray**-key-i	L. three-headed muscle of the arm
triceps surae	**tri**-seps **sir**-eye	L. three-headed muscle of the calf
triquetrum	tri-**kwe**-trum	L. three-cornered
trochanter	tro-**kan**-ter	Grk. to run
trochlea	**trok**-lee-ah	Grk. pulley
tubercle	**tu**-ber-kl	L. a little swelling
tuberosity	tu-ber-**os**-i-tee	L. a swelling
ulna	**ul**-na	L. elbow, arm
ulnolunate	**ul**-no-**lu**-nate	
ulnotriquetrum	**ul**-no-tri-**kwe**-trum	
umbilicus	um-**bil**-i-kus	L. navel, center
uvula	**uv**-u-la	L. a little grape
vastus	**vas**-tus	L. vast
vein		L. vessel
vertebra	**ver**-ta-bra	L. joint
xiphoid	**zif**-oyd	Grk. sword-shaped
zona orbicularis	**zo**-na or-**bik**-u-lar-is	L. girdle + little circle
zygomatic	**zy**-go-**mat**-ik	Grk. cheekbone
zygapophyseal	**zy**-gah-**pof**-i-se-al	

NOTES

NOTES

NOTES

Andrew Biel is a licensed massage therapist. He has served on the faculties of Boulder College of Massage Therapy and Ashmead College and has taught Cadaver Studies for Bodyworkers at Bastyr Naturopathic University. He lives outside of Lyons, Colorado with his wife, Lyn Gregory.

Shelly Loewen is a Learning Specialist, Performance Consultant and the CEO of Performance Professionals, Inc. She has a passion for learning and, since 1984, has helped companies and schools increase retention and improve the way they do business.

> Shelly Loewen, Performance Professionals, Inc.
> 9792 Edmonds Way, #412, Edmonds, WA 98020
> Phone: (206) 335-8477
> Email: saloewen@PerformanceProfessionals.com
> Web site: http://www.PerformanceProfessionals.com

Lisa Nelson serves as the Faculty Coordinator & Learning Strategist for Brenneke School of Massage and is the Principal for Updrafts Consulting. Lisa has worked in education since 1986 and applies her knowledge of learning theories, teaching methodologies and evaluation skills in ways that support student, teacher and staff success.

> Lisa Nelson, Updrafts Consulting
> 2432 - 139th St. SE, Bothell, WA 98012
> Phone: (206) 715-2835
> Email: lisannelson@yahoo.com

Robin Dorn is an artist, illustrator and licensed massage practitioner. She specializes in bodywork illustration and exhibits on the West Coast and in France.